ROUTLEDGE LIBRARY EDITIONS:
EDUCATION

THE ENGLISH EDUCATIONAL SYSTEM

THE ENGLISH EDUCATIONAL SYSTEM

G. A. N. LOWNDES

Volume 104

LONDON AND NEW YORK

First published in 1955 as '*The British Educational System*'
This edition re-issues the revised edition of 1960

This edition first published in 2012
by Routledge
2 Park Square, Milton Park, Abingdon, Oxfordshire OX14 4RN

Simultaneously published in the USA and Canada
by Routledge
711 Third Avenue, New York, NY 10017

First issued in paperback 2014

Routledge is an imprint of the Taylor and Francis Group, an informa company

© 1960 for new material G. A. N. Lowndes

All rights reserved. No part of this book may be reprinted or reproduced or utilised in any form or by any electronic, mechanical, or other means, now known or hereafter invented, including photocopying and recording, or in any information storage or retrieval system, without permission in writing from the publishers.

Trademark notice: Product or corporate names may be trademarks or registered trademarks, and are used only for identification and explanation without intent to infringe.

British Library Cataloguing in Publication Data
A catalogue record for this book is available from the British Library

ISBN 13: 978-0-415-68925-0 (Volume 104)
ISBN 13: 978-0-415-75085-1 (pbk)

Publisher's Note
The publisher has gone to great lengths to ensure the quality of this reprint but points out that some imperfections in the original copies may be apparent.

Disclaimer
The publisher has made every effort to trace copyright holders and would welcome correspondence from those they have been unable to trace.

THE ENGLISH EDUCATIONAL SYSTEM

G. A. N. LOWNDES
M.C., B. LITT., J.P.

HUTCHINSON UNIVERSITY LIBRARY
LONDON

HUTCHINSON & CO. (*Publishers*) LTD
178–202 Great Portland Street, London, W.1

London Melbourne Sydney
Auckland Bombay Toronto
Johannesburg New York

First published 1955
as 'The British Educational System'

Revised edition 1960
Second impression 1961
Third impression 1963

© for new material G. A. N. Lowndes 1960

This book has been set in Times New Roman type face. It has been printed in Great Britain by The Anchor Press, Ltd., in Tiptree, Essex, on Smooth Wove paper.

CONTENTS

Foreword   7

PART 1

CURRENT TRENDS IN ENGLISH EDUCATION

I   The primary stage of education   11
II   The secondary stage of education   30
III   Technological and further education   70
IV   The welfare services of English education and schools for the handicapped   104

PART 2

THE NATIONAL SYSTEM

V   Fundamental statistics, progress and finance   137
VI   Progress with the replacement of first-generation school buildings and the expansion of the teaching force   153
    Bibliography   177
    Index   181

FOREWORD

Most books on English education are concerned with one or more facets of the subject, express the personal standpoint of the author and assume that at least a majority of readers will be or have been engaged in some department of the educational services. This book has been expressly written for the intelligent layman or University student who may not be directly concerned with the subject, except, immediately or in the future, as a ratepayer, taxpayer and parent. It is designed to give him something more than a superficial knowledge of the relation of different parts of the English educational system to the whole; some insight into the underlying reasons for current movements of educational opinion; and the essential background to enable him to adopt a balanced personal standpoint in educational discussions.

In attempting to compress into 60,000 words a balanced picture of a subject so extensive I have had constantly in mind Thomas Love Peacock's waspish remark that education as a subject is the 'bore of all bores, with no beginning, middle or end'. Of this Sir Michael Sadler said: 'Some writers on education are dull through awkwardness with the pen. Some have turned dull through changes in the good manners of style. Some are dull because they indulge themselves in too much detail. A few can sparkle on some other subject but when they deal with education are unspeakable. Some are dull because they thought it becoming to be dull.'

Nearly twenty-five years ago I tried in a small book entitled *The Silent Social Revolution* (Oxford University Press) to show how our educational system had been built up in the years between 1895 and 1935. The impression I have gained in preparing this book is that public education in England and Wales has probably made more progress in the years since the war than that achieved in any other country except Russia and China.

FOREWORD

I should like to acknowledge the very great help I have received in compiling my material from many friends in Government Departments. The Ministry of Education, the Ministry of Health, the Registrar General and the University Grants Committee have spared no pains in supplying me with the precise statistics I have required. I am, too, deeply indebted to many colleagues in the Education Department of the County Council.

Four lines from "The Puzzler" by Rudyard Kipling are quoted on page 88 by courtesy of Mrs. George Bambridge and Messrs Macmillan & Co. Ltd.

When I was very young I was presented with a tube, in form rather like a telescope, filled with small pieces of coloured glass. When one shook it the pattern formed by the coloured pieces changed completely. It was explained to me that it had been used in a calico printing mill to help design patterns for the wood block prints. It probably was. Industrial design seemed to be of secondary importance 100 years ago when England was the workshop of the world and Lancashire could export millions of yards of printed fabrics to Africa every year though the coloured patterns disappeared 'if it so much as smelt water,' as my great aunts used to say!

I have often thought of that kaleidoscope while revising this book. The Ministries' statistics are always at least one and usually two years out of date, but, almost weekly, the unfortunate author is presented—perhaps in a Parliamentary Answer—with some new and up-to-date figure. Or a vast report like that of the Crowther Committee appears on the very day when his material goes off to the printer!

I have endeavoured throughout to present the facts, arguments and counter-arguments objectively, concealing any personal opinions I may possess. If, however, any expressions of opinion should occur I must make it plain that they should in no sense be read as implying that the London County Council accepts any responsibility for them.

G.A.N.L.

PART 1

Current Trends in English Education

I

THE PRIMARY STAGE OF EDUCATION

A PARENT'S PERPLEXITY ABOUT THE CHANGES IN THE PRIMARY SCHOOL. A TEACHER'S ANSWER. WHAT THE PRIMARY SCHOOL OF TODAY IS TRYING TO DO. HOW NEW EDUCATIONAL IDEAS ARE SPREAD.

IF THIS were a book designed for those who are actively engaged, whether as teachers or administrators, in the public service of Education it would be necessary to devote this and perhaps half a dozen succeeding chapters to an attempt to show how at the primary stage of education 'what is' is forever trying belatedly to catch up with 'what might be'; and to devote many pages to a consideration of the latest ideas in teaching methods and the achievement of a balanced timetable. Its object is, however, much more modest. Its aim is to supply the intelligent member of the public, who would like to believe that English education may not be so bad after all, with that idea of the geography of the subject, which may enable him to sift the shallow criticisms and profound nonsense too often to be met with in popular discussion and to form a judgment for himself.

Let us begin then by trying to put ourselves inside the mind of a typical modern parent, whom we will call Mrs. Everyman, and see if we can answer the question which has been forming in her mind for some time. 'How does this modern education which seems to be the rule in the primary school attended by my child and those of my neighbours compare with what we remember of our own school days? Is there not perhaps too much emphasis on freedom, too much play, too little discipline, too much movement? Is plasticine really a substitute for the six times table?'

Believing that her child must in fact get a better grounding from the well-trained and reasonably well-paid teachers at the new primary school on the housing estate than by travelling some way every day to the 'select' private school of which her mother-in-law had heard such good accounts, she has backed her own judgment and entrusted him to its care. But today her mother-in-law has come to tea and has pounced on Terry immediately he arrived home, with the inevitable inquiry, 'Well, Terry, what have you been doing at school today?' Terry, like all healthy youngsters the world over, especially when they are thinking of their tea, has roundly replied, 'Oh, nothing much.' Later, under pressure, he has admitted to having made a plasticine elephant. As soon as he has had tea and escaped to feed the rabbit Granny has shaken her head and said, 'It's all very well, my dear, for you to tell me how happy Terry is at that school and how nice the teachers are, but I am sure that when I was his age I could recite my eight times table, and his grandfather was telling me only the other day how smart he used to be at "parsing" when he can't have been much older than Terry is now.' After talking over the incident with her husband in the evening Mrs. Everyman decides to confide her troubles to Terry's teacher at the next meeting of the school's Parent Teacher Association. This, it is true, may not get her much further, because even the best of teachers would probably admit readily enough how difficult they find it to explain the whole art and mystery of their craft to others who may have been brought up in a different tradition.

Let us suppose, however, that Mrs. Everyman is lucky. It is, of course, too much to expect that any teacher, however gifted, can supply her, verbally and at a moment's notice, with a complete insight into modern trends in primary education; on the other hand, there is still a chance that after a puzzled search back into her memory over the multiplicity of things she and her class have been doing together during the term a smile of recollection may appear on the teacher's face and she may be able to say something like this: 'Oh yes, that elephant! Well, you remember we took Terry and his class to the Zoo. They were so thrilled with everything they saw that they asked whether in their next "Children's Time" they might make a Zoo for themselves in the classroom. Of course I fell in with the idea because I saw at once that it would give me precisely the chance I had been looking for to help Terry and the others to understand a bit more of the world around them: so we started by each making one or two of the animals. This naturally satisfied the delight which children of Terry's age always seem to take in using materials and becoming familiar with shapes and colours. Of course Terry is bright and I could give him the elephant to make and know he would finish it in the same time as it took some of the slower children to make less difficult animals. When we had made the animals it led naturally to finding out on the map where each animal lived; and that gave me a chance of telling the children a lot of stories about hot and cold lands and the things they produced, and the kind of people and animals that lived in them. I expect you have noticed that children of Terry's age find it much easier to understand what you and I might call "geography" than to get any idea of what you and I would call "history". Probably the pundits would say they have a better conception of "spatial" than "temporal" relations. Similarly, though they have no great power of understanding cause and effect as abstract ideas, they can see, when it is demonstrated concretely, that a polar bear must have thick fur and an elephant does not need fur at all. Next, of course, the children wanted to build the cages. We did a lot of what you used, I expect, to call "number" and Terry's Granny probably called arithmetic, in counting up the pins and matchsticks we used for railings and calculating how many we should need for each cage. We also acquired a lot of what the educationists call "manual dexterity" in cutting out and fixing up the pens and houses for the animals. Then there was all the fun we had making the "Admission Office" and discussing whether it should be sixpence for a grown-up and threepence for a child, whether brothers and sisters should be half-price, and so on. Incidentally, we covered quite a lot of what you used to call "mental sums" in the process of finding out how much visits of parties of any particular size would cost. Finally, too, we had a lot more practice in arithmetic and handwork when we came to the refreshment room. We made all the cakes, tea-cups, plates and sandwiches, and each child in turn acted as cashier, or cook, or waitress. We found it all great fun and the children loved it and really learned a tremendous amount of what you used to call geography, arithmetic, natural history, modelling and art, although, as I expect you have noticed, children of Terry's age do not divide up their insatiable curiosity into subjects.

'You will understand, I hope, that I kept a watchful eye on the whole business and the moment I felt that the intensity of the children's interest was beginning to flag the Zoo quietly disappeared and we began to explore a new field, which the class suggested as a result of my stories about Red Indians—incidentally, these started I suppose from the Zoo's buffalo! I expect you saw the class play we put on about Hiawatha? What you may not have heard about is that Terry got so thrilled when he was acting as a settler rowing a canoe faster and faster across a river to escape from the Indians that he was wet all over when he got to the other side and had to go and have a shower and change his clothes! Of course there was not really any river and we had no real canoe or paddles. It was just a piece of the playground, but that does not matter to children of Terry's age if their imagination is stirred up enough and they are really "living" a part.

'But please don't go away with the idea that Terry spends the whole of his time at school satisfying his curiosity with what may look to his Granny like unrelated snippets of knowledge which may lead to his becoming magpie-minded. Terry and his class may not realise it, but there is still such a thing as a timetable and still such a thing as a syllabus. It is my business to see that periods of "Teacher's Time" alternate with periods of "Children's Time" and that both alternate with periods when Terry and his friends are working as hard and purposefully on the drills of learning to read, to write and to deal with number as he worked on rowing his canoe. It is my business, too, to keep a careful map of the portions of the field we have explored by any particular activity such as our Zoo and to see that, by the time I pass Terry and his friends on to the next class, no part of the field—or, as we should call it, the scheme of work for the class—remains virgin territory.'

Anyone who has taken the trouble to soak himself in the written records left by the teachers of the past, or is old enough to have entered his first school at the commencement of the 20th century and yet is not too old to remember vividly the day-to-day

THE PRIMARY STAGE OF EDUCATION 15

incidents of his first few terms, will know that there were many more natural psychologists among teachers of those days than might be readily believed today. They may have used matter-of-fact language to clothe their psychological observations, saying for example that 'brothers and sisters often quarrel' when what, of course, they meant was that 'siblings frequently display a mutually antipathetic inter-relationship'!

Nevertheless, large numbers of them had an instinctive sympathy with and understanding of children; and many more of them might have been able to achieve far greater things than they, in fact, did achieve, had they not been compelled to wage an uneven battle against tightly packed classes of 60 or 70 children from homes where conversation, music, books or pictures were unknown.

By contrast the modern teacher (whether he spells Psychology with a large Ψ or merely pronounces it with an audible one!) is in fact the heir to a great deal of knowledge and understanding of the developmental needs and potentialities of children at different ages which was denied to his predecessors in earlier generations. This knowledge is, of course, not derived solely from the direct research work done by teachers, training colleges and University Institutes of Education. It has been built up, too, from the observations of doctors and psychiatrists, educational and industrial psychologists and from experience gained in colleges, schools, clinics (especially Child Guidance Clinics), offices, factories and workshops. Last, though by no means least, it derives from the patient observations of those who from being concerned vicariously with the well-being of other people's children have themselves, after marriage, compiled patient records of the behaviour, likes, dislikes and activities of their own children as they develop from year to year. The influence of all this research, disseminated through countless child welfare clinics, day nurseries, nursery and infant schools and the women's pages of newspapers and magazines, is felt in homes as well as schools and we no longer treat our children as our fathers and grandfathers were treated.

In fact many of the things which have been discovered, when stated as bald facts stripped of the language of psychology, now sound uncommonly like platitudes. So, however, do the parallel discoveries of medical science in such matters as the proper treatment of children's bodily needs. The principles painstakingly established in one generation broaden down into the truisms of the next generation but one. 'I thowt the world were over popilated' was the only response which the writer's mother could obtain from the aged grandfather of a newly born baby (which in 1904 she had found lying naked on some sacking in an empty orange box in the slum of a northern silk town) when she remonstrated with him for feeding it on 'pobs' (bread and milk).

Reduced to a single sentence then the job which the English primary school is trying to do today is to synthesise all this knowledge of child growth and behaviour into a properly conceived educational plan. This plan must be one which will draw out the unique personality of every child by presenting him with exactly the new physical, mental and aesthetic experiences and activities he needs at the precise moment, but not a minute before, he is ready to assimilate them.

Thomas Arnold, the great headmaster of Rugby, presented his child Matthew Arnold with Gibbon's *Decline and Fall of the Roman Empire* in eight volumes as a prize for his proficiency in reading at the age of two! As a good Victorian he no doubt regarded childhood as a rather tiresome, messy, irresponsible period which had to be 'got over' like the measles as quickly as possible on the way to manhood or womanhood. By contrast most people today believe that childhood is a very important part of life itself and that it is part of the child's essential birthright to be given the right chances in the right way and at the right stage in his mental as well as his physical development.

Let us take a look at some of these principles of child growth and behaviour and the more obvious repercussions which we must expect them to have upon the design, equipment and atmosphere of the good primary school community.

Before attempting to do so, however, honesty compels the writer to admit that they have been covered much more adequately and readably than by any exposition he can hope to achieve in a galaxy of Government publications and books by individual teachers of which the two which are at once the shortest, cheapest and most outstanding are the Ministry of Education pamphlet No. 15, 'Seven to eleven' and No. 14, 'Story of a school'. The unprofessional inquirer will find that these are two of the most human and readable publications which have ever been prepared in a Government Department.

Firstly then, young children may very well dislike quite heartily what we, their forerunners, probably used to call 'sums'. On the other hand, all children seem to love counting. The good primary school has not in the least forsaken the belief that knowledge of number, monetary tables, weights and measures and mastery of the skills and rules by which such knowledge is acquired and manipulated are essential for the education of any child when he is ready for each stage. Moreover, most children must eventually reach a stage when they have got to cut their teeth on what may be to them hard subjects. Where the primary school teacher today tends to break with the past is in his belief that it should not be their milk teeth that they must be compelled to cut in this way. It is comparatively easy to teach a child tricks, as for example by sheer repetition and artificial encouragement to teach him to carry out processes in Arithmetic which he does not in the least understand. Such tricks may be worse than useless to him, however, when he is required to begin serious Mathematics, because these are above all a process of reasoned deduction and logical thought. For in Primary Education a delayed start often husbands resources for the winning spurt in the last lap. It is this break with past beliefs that accounts for the fact that the visitor to the modern Infant School will no longer encounter the monotonous droning of 'tables' but will find instead groups of children handling measures, weights, cardboard money, playing shop or dominoes, throwing quoits, bowling ninepins and keeping the score. In short, they are learning, by a steady progression from counting, that a sum has actual meaning and purpose in that it is a quicker way of counting; by a steady progression from the handling of practical and concrete things to some idea, however rudimentary, of dealing with abstractions.

There are nevertheless children who appear to have as little aptitude for mathematical concepts as the tone deaf have for music. There must be many adults today who, when faced with the manipulation of any number over 10, feel themselves wishing that they could surreptitiously remove their shoes under the table! Such people must often find themselves wondering if their plight may not in reality be in part attributable to some kind of self-protective iron curtain set up in their minds by their schoolboy terror of the Mathematics teacher who tried to force them on too fast!

Secondly, young children delight in using material and arranging shapes and colours. It is the job of the primary school to give them the materials to satisfy this craving, however untidy it may appear to the casual visitor, and whatever the reactions of the school caretaker; otherwise they will be missing something essential to the development of their unique personality.

In the third place, it is the function of the good Primary teacher to ensure that the innumerable questions which a young child's limitless curiosity prompts him to ask are answered faithfully and seriously but that the answers given are 'to the question as set' and not embellished beyond the child's present degree of comprehension. There are no bounds to, but equally no compartments in, the field of the young child's inquisitiveness when it is illuminated by his sense of wonder, and few things can better develop the free use of his native tongue than 'Question Time'.

In the fourth place, young children have an insatiable urge to find things, and often this, as they grow older and begin to be able to appreciate the concept of possession, becomes a desire to collect things. It is the job of the good primary school to guide them what to look for and to show them what to collect. The transition from the belief that knowledge could be 'given' to the realisation how much better it is that it should be 'gained' is well illustrated by the contrast between the museum cupboard of the early 1900s (with its piece of desiccated sugar cane, its lump of asbestos and its stuffed seagull) and the modern nature table. This will be continuously renewed throughout the seasons. There will probably also be a bird table outside the classroom window and individual collection albums. All these require the searching out of information in the school or classroom library and more and ever more storage and classroom space. The child who has picked up an unusual leaf on the way to school and identified it in the album of pressed leaves will remember it perhaps for years. The same leaf, drawn with others on the blackboard, will probably disappear from his memory within an hour of being rubbed out.

Learning to use his eyes is, of course, for the young child the beginning of all learning. For this reason no good primary school stops at guiding its children what to look for and showing them what to collect without seeing these activities as a small part only of the much bigger task of teaching them to see and understand the world around them. By the time they are 10 or 11 this should be taking them on excursions with an object all over the area in which the school lies.

Another characteristic for which nearly all junior and most infant and nursery schools now endeavour to provide satisfaction is the young child's very special feeling of kinship with animals. This persists in some adults, though its intensity probably diminishes with the widening of the gap in mental age between, for example, the dog and its owner. Moreover, the adult's attachment to an animal is on a rational plane, while the child's response, whether it be to a favourite possession or a living creature, tends not to be primarily mental but through feeling, intuition, sensation. The population of rabbits, hamsters, guinea-pigs, hedgehogs, mice and even white and parti-coloured rats now borne on the strength of the nation's schools must be immense. Rats which are hardy, very intelligent and stand up to any amount of handling, seem to be great favourites with some schools, but non-co-operative animals like squirrels are at a discount.

It might be extremely interesting—if any such experiment were not humanly unthinkable—to amass on an electric tape recorder, and subsequently analyse, the sum total of objective knowledge possessed by, say, 500 children aged 5-11, covering a wide range of intelligence. The object of the analysis would be to trace each of the millions of items to its source and separate them into those which had become part of the child's being, and were likely therefore to remain with him for life, because he had assimilated them in response to some urge arising within himself and those which had been deliberately imparted to him from outside. The number of items on each side of the balance sheet would depend on the extent to which each child had been afforded the right environment for his development and needs in terms of experience. The balance sheet itself would probably go far to confirm a belief now widely held. This is that a child educates himself through physical movement, touch, sight, contacts, sympathies, the desire to grow up, imitation and aesthetic experiences. He learns, too, through his world of make-believe and self-dramatisation, and the correction of his own mistakes. By comparison the lessons he can be taught deliberately are far less extensive and far less permanent.

To admit that such an experiment would be impossible should not, however, absolve any potential critic of modern primary school methods from pausing to apply such a test to himself. In fact, anyone who asks himself candidly, 'How did I become what I am and develop the interests which now absorb me?' will not go far in his self-analysis without finding how often his interests as a child led by a chain of circumstances to his present interests as an adult. He will find, too, how readily even in his fifties he can recall his exasperated frustration when some well-meaning parent or teacher took the paint-brush out of his hand with the words: 'See, let me show you how to do it. I was taught to paint!'

By the end of the Junior stage of education the child of 10 or 11 is beginning to be ready for varieties of experience very different from those placed in his way at earlier ages. His first five years at school should, if they are properly employed, afford him the fundamental birthright of every child: a sense of security based on the mutual support of home and school as the two chief pillars of his life. The adventurousness of his teachers should imbue him with a feeling that school is a place where all sorts of interesting and exciting things happen and where he finds a life of his own. Where these two consummations have been achieved the last years before the secondary school claims him will witness the unfolding of a variety of new qualities. His world of make-believe will recede but he will begin to acquire some conception of time, seeing history first as the old church or castle, so different from its modern surroundings; or changes in transport through the ages. He will begin to display a sense of justice and injustice which will perhaps be developed by a wise head teacher in some form of school 'Council'. He will have passed out of the era of the common childish ailments and have achieved a sturdiness and balanced growth before the disturbances of adolescence. If his interest is enlisted his teacher will have little need to worry about 'slacking', for children of this age have been well described as 'Busy little workmen in search of jobs to do'.

He has reached a stage when there is an urge inside him to grow up and to do real work demanding effort. He will normally display no antipathy to the 'three R's', which will have come to have meaning and purpose for him as enabling him to follow up all sorts of exciting lines of inquiry for himself.

No survey however brief of the current ferment of ideas on Primary education would be complete without some mention of the revolution which modern study of child growth and behaviour is also bringing about in physical education. This revolution is the second which has taken place in this field during the past third of a century. Between the wars a system of 'leg, neck, arm, trunk' exercises interspersed with set games designed to promote the harmonious development of the body as a whole swept away the disciplined and almost military 'drill' and rigid positional exercises of an earlier era.

Since the war, however, physical education at the Infant and Junior stage has begun to display the same breakaway from any formal system of exercises performed in unison as has been witnessed in the ordinary activities of the classroom.

Here, too, the understanding visitor will find the same preoccupation with the study of the needs of growing children, the same desire to avoid expecting the child as an individual to perform feats for which he is not yet ready, the same emphasis on the value of spontaneity, exploration, liveliness, the same awareness that undue pressure to acquire technique in games may stale into boredom unless technique is allowed to develop out of play rather than precede it. He may find the class split into small groups each doing something quite different and perhaps miss those former attractive patterns produced by spread-out classes of children all performing the same movement simultaneously to the brisk commands of a teacher. He may even—if he is one of a group of spectators—have it firmly impressed upon him at the outset that he must efface himself and avoid applause. The best teachers today recoil from the idea that children's sense of drama is a fit subject to 'produce' for display and know that the natural quality in the unselfconscious dramatic movement of which quite young children are capable can easily be spoilt by awareness that they are 'on show'. In the classroom the teacher's concern is to enrich and widen the children's vocabulary, draw them out to use language flexibly, to write and speak expressively. In the physical education, dancing or games period it is to enrich and widen their experience in control over their bodies, draw them out to employ movement flexibly, and lead them to use their limbs, sense of timing and flair for dramatic and imaginative impersonation expressively.

While modern medical science and psychology have been confirming or re-examining the verdicts previously arrived at through the common sense and intuitive understanding of children possessed by teachers of earlier days, the validity of several well-entrenched educational or psychological theories of the past has inevitably been called in question. Chief among these are the 'theory of transference' and the 'theory of recapitulation of racial memories'. Mention must be made of them because in some form or other they still continually tend to crop up in educational discussions. The theory of transference was one much beloved by the classicists, the mathematicians and the school chaplains until quite late in the present century. ('Thank God I teach the Classics. They're fool-proof and don't make your fingers messy.') It postulated a belief that particular subjects could actually confer particular qualities on those who studied them instead of recognising that the qualities and aptitudes were innate and they might find their best expression along those particular lines. Thus mathematical studies were supposed to confer accuracy and attention to detail, theological studies could make a God-fearing and exemplary citizen out of the most unpromising material, while the 'grand old grind and discipline of the Classics' produced not only a grammarian but a man of judgment, an administrator and an orderly thinker. The theory is now very widely discredited, except in the sense that the mental processes demanded and mastered in the study of one subject can be applied successfully in another, if the teacher consciously teaches the transfer. There are thousands of men in their fifties who do not recognise that they owed the extreme facility with which they could as schoolboys turn out Latin or Greek verse to the same qualities as today enable them to complete *The Times* crossword puzzle in three minutes!

The theory that in their development, and particularly perhaps in their play, children recapitulate racial experience was a most attractive one. It postulated that they passed through successive stages of experimental groping towards their future status as a modern man, as cave dwellers, bushmen, hunters, members of a gang and so on. It has been so ingeniously argued, that it is hard to be told that we must discard it as belonging to an out-dated 'instinct psychology' based on 'outmoded biological speculation'.

It has been one of the misfortunes of English education that there has never been enough public money to spare in any recent decade to do more than one thing at a time really well. From 1902 to 1926 we were building our nation-wide network of secondary grammar schools. From 1926 to the outbreak of the war the Board of Education was preoccupied with the links between Technological Education and Industry on the one hand and with the creation of a place in the sun for the senior elementary school on the other. Since 1945 the long-overdue raising of the school-leaving age, the repair of our war-damaged schools and the provision of new schools on the new housing estates, particularly those required to accommodate the swollen 1943–50 age groups, have absorbed the attention of the Ministry and the Local Education Authorities. On the other hand, with this big programme of new building, and the trebling by 1959 of the intake into the Teachers' Training Colleges, the Primary stage of education, at last statutorily recognised by the Education Act of 1944 as a stage of education important in its own right, has in some respects begun to come into its own.

When the grandparents and in fact most of the parents of

today's school population were at school it was still the accepted thesis that up to the age of seven the important thing for any child was that he should be under the constant direction of a teacher. This teacher's first duty should be to maintain order as the only atmosphere in which the child could receive the instruction and learn the skills which would fit him to take his place in the junior school. Only the teacher could gauge what knowledge and skills he should possess at each stage and the techniques and devices to employ in imparting them to him. Unless the child was continually directed along these formal lines he would certainly, it was believed, get into mischief and probably grow up without knowledge or self-control. Moreover, unless the instruction appropriate to each 'Standard' had been logically presented to him in graded steps, with repeated exercises which would impress each step on his mind, he would, as likely as not, emerge at the end of his infant school course as an untidy, careless, inconsiderate youngster with no power of persistence, concentration or even the capacity to listen attentively. In short the function of the infant school was to groom and mould its children for the junior school, while that of the junior school was to groom and mould them for the senior school or, if they were exceptionally bright, for success in the highly competitive county scholarship examination for places in the local grammar school.

Thus, in many, though happily not in all, junior schools he might look forward to an unending vista of formal class teaching in which uniformity of approach was at least less conspicuous and therefore probably safer than adventurousness; the number of subjects restricted; and his progress punctuated by weekly and termly tests stimulated by rewards, marks, badges and many-hued stars ranging from the gold of extreme rectitude to the black star of punishment.

To condemn such a system out of hand would be to betray some lack of historical perspective. For, despite the loss of educational potential it involved for children whose personalities could never fully unfold under such conditions and for teachers who were forced to teach much that half their class might not be ready to assimilate, it did produce results which contributed no mean share to the winning of two wars. Moreover, the applica-

THE PRIMARY STAGE OF EDUCATION

tion of modern 'freedom and activity' methods would have been well-nigh impossible. Classes were too large, school space and the supply of equipment were often too restricted. Desks were too heavy and cumbersome. Trained teachers were usually in short supply. A high proportion of the parents were too imperfectly educated themselves—or too disinterested in anything but examination results. Had such new methods been prematurely launched in too many schools at once therefore they might have met with such a setback as to have been labelled for a generation afterwards as too whimsical to be practicable.

In education, as in other departments of national life, progressive change best consolidates itself if it starts from a number of foci of experiment. These experiments can slowly broaden out through the fertilising activities of adventurous thinkers and practitioners while remaining in touch at each stage with the findings of medical, scientific and psychological research and observation. By this means wild enthusiasm for radical changes, proper enough in the isolated enthusiast with a spark of genius, can be divested of its more unattainable extravagances. It can, too, be imitated elsewhere without provoking reaction based, for example, on some prejudice harking back perhaps to a more puritanical era when the proper concern of the schools was conceived to be solely with intellectual growth. A British Government Department which is concerned with the introduction of change in consonance with the development of national thought has two functions: firstly to collect information about all those experiments which seem beneficent until it has sufficient evidence for such changes to adopt them as a definite policy, which will be circulated to its staff in the form of procedure minutes and instructions: secondly to pull the whole hand up to the points reached by the exploring fingers. Nothing is more infectious in education than the enthusiasm of the adventurous pioneer. No Government Department has evolved a more successful corps of 'carriers' of such infection than the Ministry of Education working through Her Majesty's Inspectors of Schools.

Every H.M.I. (and they are proud of the title which for over 100 years has carried a suggestion of direct appointment by the Sovereign in order to preserve the independence of their advice to the Minister) will have been picked from a field of at least 100 successful teachers. As a body they would be the last to claim that in this matter of fertilisation of new ideas and techniques as they go from school to school they have a monopoly. A great number of short refresher courses are arranged both by the Ministry and the Local Education Authorities every year to familiarise teachers with original developments in other schools. The educational press, too, for long concerned with professional matters, has changed out of recognition in the past 30 years in its desire to assist teachers in their actual school work and by reporting successful experiment. Finally assistant teachers who have given the lead in experimenting widely and wisely with such ideas in due course become heads. The freedom enjoyed by the British head teacher in the choice of books and material, the preparation of the syllabus and the guidance of teaching methods in his or her school is at once the envy of other countries and the essential launching platform for educational innovations.

Thus, soon after the First World War, Margaret McMillan* and other nursery school pioneers by their experiments established in an English setting, and with an English twist, Madame Montessori's principle that the child will grow naturally and educate himself spontaneously—impelled by forces within himself—if given an environment suitable for his developmental needs. The validity of the experimental work and ideas developed in the first nursery schools spread upwards to the infant schools. There, too, it soon came to be realised that the child of five to seven watching the grown-up occupations of others in his house dramatised himself in his play as imitating such occupations for himself. It followed that for a child of this age to garden, arrange flowers and care for pets might be far more educative than a formal nature lesson. Again to talk spontaneously to the teacher and other children while other activities of many kinds were in progress might give him far more poise and control of his native tongue than a 'conversation lesson'. Similarly, to paint from imagination pictures he really wanted to paint might carry him forward far more rapidly in acquiring manual skill and appreciation than drawing from models or learning to make formal patterns or design. The 'three R's' might be acquired much more

THE PRIMARY STAGE OF EDUCATION 27

naturally if he were surrounded by attractive books, notices and labels in the classroom. Such books might excite a natural desire to read them or himself write messages he wished to send. Finally, a supply of games with a purpose involving scoring, counting, playing at shop might entice him to take his first steps in number, perhaps on the classroom floor, far more readily than if he were compelled to sit immobile at a desk and watch the teacher writing symbols on a blackboard.

It is, however, extraordinarily difficult to arrive at any satisfactory answer if anyone asks the very natural questions: What proportion of the nation's schools at each level has, in fact, accepted wholeheartedly and put into practice the ideas outlined in the preceding pages? What proportion is experimenting with them? What proportion adheres to the more formal approach and teaching techniques of pre-war days?

It is clear that they have won wholehearted acceptance throughout the nursery schools. They have found warm adherents, too, among Her Majesty's Inspectors of Schools. Here, however, one will encounter the very proper reservation that such methods can put such a tax on the energies of any teacher and make such heavy demands on his or her capacity for sustained originality, adaptability and adventurousness that it is better for a weak or unconvinced teacher to adhere to formal methods. They have won over the Teachers' Training Colleges, particularly those training teachers for work with nursery, infant and the younger junior children. It is interesting to find that such colleges can at present normally hope to place at least half their trainees at schools where the methods they have learnt will be exactly what their first head teacher wants.

By inference, therefore, it may possibly be argued that they have affected at least half of the infant schools, particularly perhaps those where new ideas can find a space to spread their roots in new buildings. Clearly, too, they have modified to a greater or lesser degree the practice of a substantial proportion of the remainder of the infant schools.

At the junior school stage they meet with a check. This is not necessarily because the heads or their teaching staffs are hostile or unreceptive. It needs a great deal of courage on the part of newly appointed junior school heads, and a serene conviction that they can rely on the support and backing of their Managers, the Local Education Authority and their Inspectors, to adopt teaching methods to which the parents of children who fail to secure grammar school places in the common entrance test at 11 are bound to attribute that failure.

Any teacher who has worked in a junior school in one of the few areas where there is no common entrance test will know how the whole educational atmosphere of the school can be uplifted by the freedom it enjoys to let its activities burgeon unshadowed by an approaching examination. At the other end of the scale, and lest it be thought that in an attempt to correct the too frequent denigrations of English primary schools this chapter has painted too rosy a picture, it is unfortunately necessary to admit that there are still many hundreds of dreary little primary schools both in town and country where the atmosphere still appears to be as impervious to new ideas as the Managers are to the need for structural improvements. Unfortunately, too, most Training College Principals still from time to time encounter cases where an intelligent and enthusiastic student trained in the new methods is warned on arrival in her first post that she had better forget much that she has learnt at Training College. It is hard to imagine anything more dispiriting for the keen probationer or more wasteful to the taxpayer, some £1000 of whose money has probably been spent on her training. Crabbed age should always be careful in administering warnings to youth and recall that the young are always right—if only because they will write the history books about us after we have gone!

One inevitable result of the new emphasis on activity methods in the Training Colleges has been that the new teacher normally specialises to a greater extent than in the past on the most appropriate methods of teaching children within a narrow age range. She will no longer be trained to become a general subjects teacher of children of all ages but a nursery-trained, infant-trained, Junior-trained teacher and so on. This led to a growing realization that the two years' training was really too short. Indeed, once the educational world ceased to think of teachers as though they were static 'hands' working the pumps at a filling station and came to regard their jobs as that of a skilled test mechanic at the wheel of someone else's precious machine with its delicate and easily damaged mechanism the extension of the teachers' period of training to three years became inevitable. This is a reform which is due to begin in September 1960. The possibility of applying it successfully will depend upon continued attraction into the profession of the requisite number of secondary school leavers of the right calibre. It is to be hoped that ample opportunities will be afforded to those teachers who have carried the burden of the post-war 'bulge' to take a third-year course of training on full pay and perhaps in preparation for work with a different age group.

*p.26: Margaret McMillan did not copy Madame Montessori's methods although both owed something to Séguin, the French educational writer. Madame Montessori's concern was to evolve for educationally sub-normal children a range of educational apparatus to be worked through on a 'cycle' plan, each cycle repeating the former exercises but becoming progressively more difficult. Miss McMillan felt this system did not train the young child's imagination sufficiently and her teachings and practice are now more generally followed in England than Madame Montessori's.

II

THE SECONDARY STAGE OF EDUCATION

WHY A BREAK AT 11? THE FUNCTION OF SECONDARY EDUCATION. WHAT ARE THE PROPER OBJECTIVES OF SECONDARY EDUCATION IN BRITAIN'S POST-WAR WORLD? THE SECONDARY GRAMMAR SCHOOL. THE SECONDARY TECHNICAL SCHOOL. THE SECONDARY MODERN SCHOOL. MISGIVINGS ABOUT THIS TRIPARTITE MOULD. EXPERIMENTS TO MEET THESE MISGIVINGS. THE '18 PLUS' PROBLEM.

ABOUT the age of 11, 83 children in England and Wales out of every 100 in the total age group of 629,000 now pass out of the primary schools into one of the wide variety of secondary schools. Of the remaining 17, 7 stay in unreorganised schools, which are often those controlled by the religious denominations or sometimes those serving country parishes too remote for the children to be picked up and conveyed to the nearest secondary school even by the ubiquitous school bus. It is now one of the first objectives of national policy to eliminate these all-age schools as quickly as possible. The remaining ten will be in private schools outside the public system of education or in special schools for the handicapped.

Why, it may legitimately be asked, is a change of such importance made so early as 11? The honest answer is that there is no magic, either educational, psychological or physiological, in the choice of this age. In a perfectly organised society the transfer might indeed with advantage be postponed for a year or, better still, two years, as in fact it is in the case of the change from the private preparatory to the private boarding schools. Such a society may eventually come to pass. It will, however, have to be one far less trammelled by economic necessities than is still the case today. All children will have to be able to stay in full-time schools as long as they can profit by it. All primary schools will have to be as good as the best now existing.

The real reasons are to be sought in a blend of administrative and educational convenience with a backward glance at past social conditions and beliefs.

The minimum school leaving age up to 1947 was the end of the term in which a child reached his fourteenth birthday. It was not until 1947 that the end of the term in which he reached his fifteenth birthday was substituted. Transfer at 13 would therefore have allowed far too short a secondary school career for the great mass of the country's children.

From an educational standpoint the gap between one child and another created by differing aptitudes for academic studies widens with every year of age. Thus differences barely noticeable on entry to the primary school e.g. between two children who, on their respective fifth birthdays, had mental ages of four and six might, by their tenth birthday, have doubled to mental ages of 8 and 12. At this point the two children would clearly require to be taught by different methods or at a different pace. This was becoming more and more difficult to achieve in the small all-ages schools of the pre-1926 era from which barely one child in twenty in those days passed at 11 with a scholarship to the local grammar school.

The 'Hadow' Report of the Consultative Committee of the Board of Education which in 1926 recommended the 'break at eleven' coincided with a great development of country bus services and an enormous growth of new housing estates. These estates with adjacent villages served by the new bus routes normally produced a sufficient child population of 11 and upwards to justify the provision of two sizeable senior elementary schools. In the social conditions of those days it was often thought desirable to plan one school for each sex. This was justified by the plea that it would facilitate planning for the somewhat different educational needs of boys and girls. A further justification was found in the theory that the psychological and physiological changes of adolescence rendered the task of the secondary school teacher considerably more difficult than that of the teacher of primary age children or adults. Single sex education it was argued would reduce the difficulty of finding appropriate teachers. Under the improved social conditions of today many experienced teachers would probably reject this thesis as exaggerated and see in co-education a means of resolving more difficulties in the future of adolescent boys and girls than they are likely to experience in their present.

Many would go further and suggest that the authors of the Hadow report, and the Norwood report which supplemented it, were led, whether by design or accident, into stressing those arguments which tended to rationalize and support the theory that the child population could be neatly divided into three distinct types so early as the eleventh year.

This was a convenient gospel thirty years ago when the mass of the nation's children left school at the end of the term in which their fourteenth birthday occurred; when a large proportion of that mass was older, in a worldly sense, than its counterpart of today; and when most people believed without question that 'intelligence' and 'bents' were constant properties which could be accurately diagnosed by the time a child reached eleven and were unamenable to radical alteration by parental encouragement, good home influences, improved health and dogged qualities of character in the individual.

To distinguish between the *function* of the secondary stage of education as conceived in England by contrasting it with that of the primary stage is comparatively easy. To isolate and set down on paper any definitive statement of its *objectives*—true for every decade and every environment—is well-nigh impossible.

The essential difference in *function* is that the primary school supplies the first tools of learning. It awakens the first aesthetic experience. It begins the unfolding of an ethical consciousness by guiding and using the young child's innate feeling for justice and fair play. It employs as stimulants to enrich his experience his sense of wonder, interest in finding, making, matching, exploring and arranging things, his feelings of affinity with animals and his joy in movement, miming and simple music.

The secondary school, it is true, continues this process of integration of personality and self-realisation. But it does so on an increasingly intellectual level—albeit with the realisation that at some point, according to the place of each individual on the waveband of academic aptitude, a law of diminishing returns will begin to operate. Initially its technique is to seek to substitute for the mere acquisition of uncorrelated knowledge a desire to test, to question, and later to reason about, that knowledge, so that, in due course, it may all be assimilated into the personality. In the process it attempts to guide the adolescent to acquire personal, moral and social values. It tries to encourage him to recognise the milestones—cultural, scientific, constitutional, religious—along mankind's progress to destiny. Thus it is during this second stage of a boy's or girl's education that observant teachers and parents should progressively begin to discern the future pattern of the man or woman whose character they have been helping to unfold.

Nevertheless they will be wise to keep a wary eye open for the 'diminishing returns', the signs of which are increasingly broad patches of partial comprehension leading to boredom, and, before these proceed too far, endeavour to pass the pupil to some alternative form of education such as apprenticeship with part-time day release. Every good secondary school will, however, bend all its energies to produce in the highest possible proportion of its pupils, before the doors of the school close behind them, a respect for scientifically proved fact and some capacity to distinguish between what is good and what is meretricious in art, music, films, wireless and television programmes. Boys or girls who have received a good secondary education will carry into life as the hallmark of their schooling a perpetual question mark above their heads and, when afforded a brief opportunity for leisure, a desire to pick up a book which will stretch their powers rather than act as a sedative or an escape.

To set down on paper what should be the proper *objectives* of a nation-wide attempt to give secondary education appropriate to the 'age, aptitude and attainment' of every child is a very different task. Anyone who tries to do this will, if he is wise, soon come to realise that anything he may write today will probably be out of date almost before the ink is dry.

To their credit, this has not deterred numerous private individuals, many of them with great experience, from contributing their personal viewpoint to swell the output of Royal Commissions, consultative committees and *ad hoc* inter-departmental working parties. In almost every case, however, what they have written will appear to the next body in the field to have dated, to have overstressed one aspect or to have under-estimated the importance of another.

The explanation probably lies not only in the accelerated tempo of social, economic, political and artistic thought and change over the past 50 years—in which, of course, the rise of public education has itself been a major factor—but in the similarly increasing tempo of changes in the schools themselves. The picture of public education before the eyes of the Royal Commission on Secondary Education, which sat under the chairmanship of Lord Bryce in 1895, was something utterly different from that which confronted the framers of the Education Act of 1944. Nevertheless, Lord Bryce and his colleagues reached out in imagination to a definition of the proper objectives of secondary education far nearer to our modern conceptions than many of their successors.

To the Mid-Victorian, secondary education had been a 'high word', the preparation for knowledge and the imparting of knowledge in proportion to that preparation. It had not been conceived of as a second stage in the education of a whole people. It had been a type of education reserved, like the first- and second-class carriages on the Victorian railway system, for the favoured few; for those, in fact, who would in Church and State, in the Law and the Services, on the Bench and from country estates, exemplify the national ideal of the gentlemanly amateur 'all-rounder'.

Just in time the country realised that its future in the first half of the new century would probably depend on school power as well as sea power. Unfortunately it did not reach this realisation through the minds of those who, at the time, controlled national policy. Thus the foresight of men like Sir Michael Sadler, who saw with clear eyes the educational and economic advance in the other countries of Western Europe and the United States, the social awareness of such political administrators as Mr. Sidney Webb and the idealism of thinkers of the stamp of Professor R. H. Tawney were to some extent side-tracked.

Those who advised the Minister of the day were products of the academic traditions of Winchester and New College, Oxford, and thought it right to put all the money available into providing a nation-wide network of secondary grammar schools when they might have done better to put half of it into secondary technical schools.

In retrospect we can now see that this was probably the greatest mistake in English educational history.

What is not in doubt, however, is the commendable speed with which, in a couple of generations, our reserves of adequately educated man and woman power were multiplied to something like 15 times those existing at the opening of the new century. The gentlemanly amateur, who learned on the playing-fields of Eton to officer the uncomplicated armies of Waterloo, gave place first to the product of the little asphalt yards and playgrounds of our pre-1914 elementary and secondary schools who endured the long-drawn, muddy stalemates of the 1914–18 war. A generation later, between 1939 and 1945, the classrooms of our secondary and technical schools were able to provide the unending stream of experts, both men and women, without whose trained or trainable intelligence Britain would have been overwhelmed. These were the men and women who manned the planes, guns, Radar and degaussing installations, the electricians, coppersmiths, signallers, sea and army cooks, engineers on landing craft, skilled cinema operators, modern language experts, welfare workers in shelter and factory, civil nursing and child care reservists.

Thus it was quite natural for a Member of the House of Commons to assert during the passage of the Education Act, 1944, that 'The people of this country can regard themselves as having been paid back every penny they ever spent on their education rate by what happened in the skies of Britain between June and September 1940.' It was quite natural, too, for Sir Winston Churchill to say in one of his wartime broadcasts to the nation, 'I believe that if we are to survive and prosper as a nation, it is going to be very important that we should be a well-educated nation.'

Where, then, does our thought about secondary education stand today as we move forward into the second half of the 20th century?

Two world wars within our lifetime have taught us as a people to believe in the training of intelligence as a right at whatever level it is found in a way in which we certainly did not believe in it during the early decades of the century. Moreover, we have had a grim warning of the fate which must in the future overwhelm any people whose rulers believe that they can truncate the top forms of their secondary schools and put their scientists not into laboratories but into uniform.

When taking stock of our own position, we are clear-sighted enough to see that, with our foreign investments sold to pay for our survival, we are facing the following situation.

(a) In the economic sphere we are a small island with a teeming population not capable of supporting itself from its own agricultural production. Thus, we shall need to produce, through our secondary schools, the maximum possible supply of highly skilled workers and technologists whose minds have been unlocked by their education, not merely stored with uncorrelated knowledge. Only so can we maintain, let alone improve, our standard of life. For this will involve the production, at competitive prices, of goods of better quality, craftsmanship and design, greater durability and precision than our industrial competitors in the rest of the world.

(b) In the sphere of natural resources and transport we are a country with few present alternative sources of power to coal and little natural oil. It is thus vital to our interests that our schools and universities should give us the physicists capable of exploring the new vistas opened up by the early industrial development of nuclear energy. In addition we shall need scientists and technologists capable of exploiting to the full firstly the accident of geography which has placed us at the hub of the air routes linking the greatest present centres of world population; secondly the industrial applications of science unknown to the pre-war textbooks—for example ultrasonics, electronics and isotopes.

(c) In the sphere of political thought we are a nation which has hitherto been more successful in establishing the democratic way of life than in ensuring that its citizens appreciate the responsibilities entailed in the maintenance of that way of life. We must therefore look to our schools to turn out men and women who carry individually a question mark of such dimensions above their respective heads as to make it unlikely that they will be seduced in large numbers by propaganda designed to persuade them to adopt some other system.

(d) In the sphere of social development we are a country with an educational system hitherto moulded largely by history and tradition formed at the time when we were still a wealthy country—the workshop of the world—with a far greater social stratification than today. Now we suddenly find ourselves at the commencement of 'the century of the common man'. This creates a situation in which thoughtful parents of today have a clear claim to be given education for their children better, if possible, than they themselves received. All such parents now have at least two generations of educated forbears and all of them, by their conduct in the Second World War, have deserved well of their fellow countrymen. Nothing short of an education which will fit their children to obtain and fill the highest posts to which their intelligence entitles them is going to satisfy these modern parents. This postulates a vast and rapid expansion of that equality of opportunity through education towards which we have been working since the century opened.

Is this a just appraisal of this country's post-war situation and what it will require of its schools and universities? If it is, that situation is clearly going to call for the evolution of a system of secondary education for all to the very limit of the capacity of each. It must surely, too, be a system which must set its sights beyond those neatly rounded definitions which seemed so satisfying to earlier generations. Anyone who has attended school speech days will recall such definitions as 'the fully integrated and balanced individual', 'the cultured personality in whose presence others will weigh their words before they speak', 'the mind liberalised by the discipline of its faculties', 'one who is enlightened in his interests, impersonal in his judgments, ready in his sympathy for whatever is just and right, effective in the work he sets himself to do and willing to lend a hand to anyone who is in need of it'. Are they any longer adequate to this new Elizabethan age, and the new Industrial Revolution upon which we are entering?

This tendency to weigh in the balance past efforts to define secondary education and, in the light of present-day conditions, to find something wanting in each undoubtedly explains the anxious questionings in staff common rooms and their echoes in the Press. It explains, too, the tendency among many of the most experienced thinkers, lecturers and writers on educational subjects to emphasise that in our modern world it is not sufficient to educate men and women for the good life without at the same time seeking to educate them to accomplish something in that good life. They accept without reservation the thesis that secondary education should enrich its recipient as a person and point his way to responsible citizenship. Nevertheless, they are becoming ever more convinced that it must also be a pursuit of intellectual training and personal discipline conducted with a special view to the kind of profession or occupation in which men and women aim to make their personal contribution to their time and generation.

No sooner, of course, do members of local education authorities, teachers, inspectors or educational administrators begin to think along these lines than some at least of them also begin to question whether they have not been too rigid hitherto. They have forced 83% of the children of England and Wales into a three-tier mould of grammar, secondary technical and secondary modern schools at the early age of 11. Have they provided enough opportunities for them to pass at a later stage from one section of the mould to another? Has not one obvious result been that many border-line children have been excluded who might have profited more by the grammar school course than some of those just above the line whose instability or unsatisfactory home conditions caused them to leave school at 15 or 16? What is the remedy for another obvious result, the general dissatisfaction on the part of parents not only with the selection itself but with the disturbance caused to children in the later stages of their primary school course by the shadow of the approaching selection examination?

THE SECONDARY STAGE OF EDUCATION 39

Inevitably cracks have begun to appear in the three-tier mould and these show every sign of widening as one Local Education Authority after another applies its collective ingenuity to working out local solutions promising greater flexibility.

Before proceeding further with a discussion of these developments, however, it may be well to give some outline of the distinctive features of the three main types of school—secondary grammar, secondary technical and secondary modern as they still exist. For this tripartite division will certainly continue to cover the major part of the educational field for the next 20 years, although there are already signs that the three types are tending to develop overlaps.

The secondary grammar schools in England and Wales now number in round figures 1,665, with 42,000 staff and 770,000 pupils. (These figures include, as they clearly must, all those schools which are financially outside the national system but are recognised by the Ministry of Education as efficient secondary schools.)

Overall, they at present represent the most homogeneous type of secondary school, in the sense that a visitor who was blindfolded and allowed to sit for a day in a dozen classrooms containing, say, pupils of 14 at a dozen different secondary schools of the three main types, would probably find a greater similarity in what he heard in the 12 grammar schools than in either of the other groups. This is not a criticism, it is merely another way of saying that the grammar school curriculum has been, if not moulded, at least conditioned by the preparation of its pupils for the General Certificate of Education, normally taken about the age of 16. This is intended to confer on the pupil of that age the cachet of having satisfactorily completed a five-year course of secondary education.

Their function is described by the Ministry, in their attractive pamphlet 'The New Secondary Education', as follows:

> 'The grammar school offers a general course lasting for about five years in which the treatment of all subjects and groups of subjects, but notably languages (classical and modern), mathematics and science, follows a predominantly

logical development, and a subsequent intensive course in the sixth form covering a narrower range of subjects which, for many boys and girls, leads naturally on to studies at the university level. The distinguishing feature of both courses lies not so much perhaps in their content as in their length, in the scholarly treatment of their content and in the stern intellectual discipline that they afford.'

In seeking the causes of their undoubted success and the standing which they have built up in the minds of parents, it is a mistake to assume that this is merely based on the social prestige which, like the older foundations on which they were modelled, they are supposed to confer. Too many critics of the old school tie overlook the fact that the secondary grammar school course is the recognised path leading to a large group of professional occupations. Moreover, the number of such occupations has increased enormously in a society moving from the unspecialised and undifferentiated to the specialised and differentiated.

	Census 1891	*Census 1931*	*Census 1951*
Professional occupations	507,870	746,085	1,386,600
Commercial occupations	416,365	2,071,420	2,230,100

The attitude of most wise parents would be 'social prestige no doubt makes one feel good, but a sound job lasts a lifetime!' Anyone who is tempted, therefore, to bury himself in his morning paper when a proud parent begins to tell the railway carriage at large of his son's success at the local grammar school might spare a moment to enumerate mentally the wish-fulfilments of his own frustrated youth, which he has experienced vicariously in the success of his own children.

A bird's-eye survey of the 1,665 grammar schools to compare them with the 3,690 modern schools would also leave an overwhelming impression of the advantages they still enjoy, and are likely to continue for many years to come to enjoy, in all such visible evidences of a well-found school as playing fields, assembly halls, gymnasia, libraries, science laboratories, swimming-baths, furnishings, equipment and visual aids. Although the Ministry of

Education regulations covering the provision of all such amenities now make virtually no distinction between one type of secondary school and another, parity of provision, the first step towards parity of esteem, will take many years. Some magnificent new secondary modern schools have, however, been built since the war—notably that at Wokingham in Berkshire—and many more will have been erected before 1961, by which date the secondary school roll will probably be at its maximum (owing to the birth-rate of the years 1943–49). The story of the headmaster of an ancient grammar school who was found staggering away from the opening ceremony of one such palatial new modern school murmuring brokenly, 'Parity of treatment, my foot!' is probably apocryphal, and certainly, as yet, far from typical.

The strictly intellectual achievements of the secondary grammar schools are impressive enough. The scholarships, exhibitions, university prizes and subsequent distinctions which their products win at the universities are increasing annually. It is probable that they are every year, too, carrying a higher number of their pupils to a better standard of achievement, but the substitution of the General Certificate of Education at ordinary and advanced level for the former School Certificate and Higher School Certificate which were not of quite so high a standard makes a comparison at present difficult. With this reservation it may be noted that as against 427,000 passes in subjects at the ordinary level in the General Certificate of Education in its first year 1951 there were 748,000 in 1958. At Advanced level the number of passes in individual subjects was 76,300 in 1950. This had become 120,300 by 1958 and probably the 150,000 figure will be found to have been reached in the summer of 1959.*

Apart from their standards of scholarship, however, there are other important features which are too often taken for granted by parents and staff. These seldom fail to evoke praise from American, French or German teachers who spend a few terms on their staff as 'exchange' teachers. The free but respectful relationship between staff and children is a point usually singled out for favourable comment. American teachers are also impressed by the sensible admixture of school work, physical training and games (for every boy and girl, not merely for those who are likely to win credit for the school if coached for a team). Again the English secondary grammar schools present a unity in variety in such activities as dramatic work, school societies, educational visits and school journeys. This often appears particularly striking to the teacher from Continental countries who has perhaps hitherto only known the rather rigid relationship and pursuit of erudition in the secondary school which draws its inspiration from some Teutonic model, or the rather formal and logical pursuit of learning for its own sake in the French *lycée*.

There are, indeed, those who would give almost as high a place as they do to the academic achievements of these schools to what might be described as their 'invisible exports'. The English secondary school, they argue, offers to the boy or girl a chance to develop far more qualities of spirit and character, and far more important qualities, too, for their lives and those of others about them, than can ever be tested by public examinations. For no examination can test a man or woman's sense of humour; his or her capacity to get on with fellow men and women in every walk of life; his or her capacity for the kind of leadership which ensures co-operation by inspiring it. No examination paper is devised to reveal the future saint or mystic. Yet it is arguable that it is precisely the men and women who possess these qualities who make a far greater contribution to their respective time and generation than the captains and the kings.

The first point which it is often necessary to emphasize in regard to the *Secondary Technical School* is that it is not a 'technical' school at all. For a technical school proper seeks to teach a trade or prepare its students for entry to or success in a specific occupation. Nor is it a school providing a general secondary education with technical studies added. It is in fact a school which gives a first-class secondary education by using the strongly marked interest of its pupils in some definite field of human activity as the 'vitamin' or catalyst to break down what might otherwise prove a diet of general principles too rich or abstract for their proper assimilation. There is no reason, for instance, why it should not turn a boy, if he is of the bent of mind appropriate to its curriculum, into a better clergyman than he might have been had he followed the traditional grammar school course, even though it may have used an initial interest in engineering or building as the means to unlock his mind.

In other words, it is the school *par excellence* for the boy or girl of good intelligence who by the end of the junior school course is beginning to display a more than average fascination for scientific phenomena; a strongly marked urge to explore things structural or mechanical; a well-developed sense of fitness, aesthetic or practical, in fine needlecraft, good design, sound craftsmanship, good cooking; an awareness of that romance of commerce epitomised in Rudyard Kipling's *Big Steamers*.

Most honest teachers of the upper forms of junior schools would probably admit that 11 is too early an age for them to diagnose such bents with absolute certainty, although they will often be helped in doing so by their knowledge of the home or discussion with the parents. Still less can they hope to avoid a proportion of their more intelligent children obtaining borderline places in the selection test for the grammar school where their subsequent development makes it clear that they would have done far better to have joined a secondary technical school. For these reasons there is much to be said for the idea of combined grammar-technical schools.

For the first two years in the secondary technical school (11 to 13+) the curriculum would probably not in fact appear to the outside observer to differ very markedly from that in the secondary grammar school. There would, for instance, be the same emphasis on the basic skills, the Arts, Science and probably a second language. Where the informed observer would probably notice a subtle difference would be in the skill with which the staff (normally men and women with considerable experience, before taking up teaching, in one of the groups of industries or commercial avocations to which the school points) would use the pupil's known interests as a stimulant to purposeful work; and the watch they would maintain on their practical and handwork as providing the best pointers to the kind of career at which they might best aim.

During the next two years (13+ to 15+) it normally becomes possible for the staff to diagnose with some certainty what particular group of activities (still used, it should be remembered, as a catalyst) is likely to suit any given boy or girl. At this stage transfers should be arranged to other schools which have built their curriculum around those activities, if the school in which the first two years have been spent does not provide them.

That fundamental of crowd psychology that no crowd likes to decrease its numbers is still, unfortunately, responsible for many educational misfits through reluctance to transfer a boy or girl who may be giving much to a school in other respects. This is yet another argument for comprehensive or Bi-lateral schools large enough to offer a variety of options without transfers.

From 13+ to 15+ the vitamin dosage is increased and the equivalent of at least a full session a week will be spent in an introduction to technology or commercial subjects or whatever the speciality of the school may be. To an increasing degree, too, the Science, the Art, the History, the Geography and the Languages will be influenced by that speciality.

At 15+ it is normally possible to make the final decision as to the type of career in which the pupil should commence. For example, at 16+ he might enter upon a craft (or student) apprenticeship, or an office linked with works apprenticeship. Alternatively he might take the General Certificate of Education and follow full- or part-time study at a Technical College leading to one of the National Certificates awarded by the Professional Bodies in Civil, Mechanical, Chemical, Production or Electrical Engineering, Chemistry, Applied Physics, Applied Chemistry, Metallurgy, Building, Commerce, Textiles, Naval Architecture, Mining or Retail Distribution. A proportion of Secondary Technical Scholars will reach the Universities.

The greatest strength of the secondary technical school is the purposeful keenness of every pupil. Boredom, the greatest brake on educational progress, finds little or no place in it and the casual visitor need never expect to become an object of interest to any classroom he may enter. Its product spans the gap between the professional man or woman drawing inspiration from thought expressed on an academic plane through the printed word, and the worker at the bench or counter.

The failure to provide sufficient secondary technical schools *pari passu* with the creation of the national network of grammar schools in the years when building labour was both cheap and available is now regarded by nearly all informed educational opinion as the great 'might have been' of English education. It is a deficiency which at whatever cost we shall be wise to repair in the next 20 years, for at present there are only 284 secondary technical schools with about 98,300 pupils (if one includes those in 38 Bilateral and Multilateral schools). Since, however, the Secondary Technical School, as we shall see in the next Chapter, probably has the finest record of any type of school in the production of the Technologists and Technicians which the country needs so vitally, it is encouraging to note that the present attendance is 25,000 greater than it was barely eight years ago.

The 3,690 *secondary modern schools* constitute the third section of the tripartite mould and into this section about 56 in every 100 children who leave the Junior Schools at 11 are at present poured. This type of Secondary School is regarded by the keen and experienced head teacher as a challenge; by the parent of the Junior School child too often as a cloud marring the bright horizon of his 'hopeful'; and by the shallow intellectual snob as a repository for 'duffers'.

Inevitably these schools must draw from a broader section of the wave-band of academic aptitude than either the secondary grammar or the secondary technical school. At the one end they will receive the boy or girl who has been unlucky—perhaps through difficult home conditions or persistent ill-health—in the selection test at 11. These may very well emerge with flying colours from the 'late developers' test now arranged by most Local Education Authorities to pick up such children at the age of 12 or 13.

At the other end they have to do the best they possibly can for the boys or girls whose mental processes are so slow, or so involved, that it will be lucky if by the end of their schooldays they can do more than read a sentence of single-syllable words with sufficient comprehension of its sense, when they reach the end of it, to detect an obvious improbability in it. An example of such a sentence would be: 'I got on a train with my aunt and in an hour we came to a town where we found a boat. We got in the boat and rowed back home in five minutes.' As an example of a child at the other end of the wave-band compare the 10-year-old girl who, asked to put 'true', 'false' or 'I cannot say' against a number of statements, encountered the sentence, 'When I woke up on Christmas morning, I was not surprised to find snow on the ground.' 'It all depends,' she replied. 'I should have been very surprised, I expect, if I had been living in Australia!' She won her place in a Grammar School!

A fact which is not even today nearly sufficiently widely appreciated is that in every 1,000 children there may be (if one includes the ineducable and the educationally sub-normal) as many as 25[1] who are unable to read and comprehend, for example, the Beacon Book Four; or whose grasp of the written word is so tenuous that they will have forgotten how to read by the time they are examined on call-up for National Service. This is a tragic waste of human material. More serious still, it is from this group that a large amount of juvenile delinquency may arise—unless it is countered by the esprit de corps which the best type of secondary modern school will foster.

Moreover, the ability to read and do simple calculations is much more important than it was for example to the Ortherises or Mulvaneys of Kipling's India. Deficiencies which probably passed unnoticed in those roistering worthies cause much well-publicised consternation to senior officers in the Services today and inevitably 'hit the headlines' in the daily press when some illiterate young desperado appears before the Courts.

More could no doubt be done to improve the performance of the borderline readers if enough teachers were available to afford them special tuition in small groups. Yet it is grossly unfair to suggest that a state of affairs which arises primarily from a distribution of natural ability that has probably not changed since the time of Plato is due to bad teaching. It is equally foolish to forget that, on the other side of the balance sheet, this country was demonstrated in 1950 to be easily the most literate of the thirty-six examined by Unesco in such matters as the production

---

[1] Of 6,125 school leavers in one year in the West Riding, 188 were in this category, but tests carried out by the Army in 1951–52 revealed only 7 per 1,000 unable to read better than a child of seven.

THE SECONDARY STAGE OF EDUCATION 47

of books and the number of newspapers read per head of the population.

On the assets side, the secondary modern school does start with one substantial advantage. The pupils need not spend their schooldays, like those at secondary grammar schools or in the upper forms of the junior schools, under the shadow of an examination. Every pupil can therefore be regarded by a keen Head and an alert staff as a 'Bank' of potentialities out of which they must endeavour to draw the maximum which he is capable of yielding, instead of their being obliged to ask themselves, at increasingly frequent intervals as the examination approaches, how his account stands.

The staff of a secondary modern school are probably able on this account to interest themselves more than those at either of the other types of secondary school in the all-round development, mental, moral and physical, of the 'whole' pupil as distinct from the intellectual progress of the whole group, form or set. There is indeed something very exhilarating in the way the Head of a good modern school will talk not of his brighter pupils as a class but of some particular boy who seemed hopeless, and was quite unable to read, until at 13 he suddenly discovered a sense of achievement in the Art room. Perhaps for the first time in his life this earned him praise and encouragement, and seemed to unlock his mind so suddenly that he learnt to read with a rush. Or he will point with pride to 'that grand chap over there' who helped to build the greenhouse with the glass partitions salved from the bombed section of the school, has kept the seed-trays filled and the school herbaceous border stocked ever since and is now determined, with the help of the Y.M.C.A., to become a farmer. The pride of the good modern school Head in his geese who have become swans, his school's clean bill of health with the Juvenile Court, the keenness shown by the emergency trained member of his staff, the number of boys or girls who want to remain for another year or two after 15, is in fact one of the most heartening things in English education today.

It all comes back to the degree to which the staff of such schools have been prepared to combat boredom and stimulate hard and purposeful work through the discovery of interesting activities which give the pupils a sense of having achieved something worth while for themselves and of their own volition.

Undoubtedly the school which succeeds in doing this will soon develop in its upper forms something of the intensity of purpose met with in the secondary technical school—albeit on a slightly lower intellectual plane. For working through a broad and balanced curriculum rendered realistic by a wide variety of practical activities it will have given every pupil some clearly defined aim within his or her reach. In doing so it will have led the parents to appreciate that failure to achieve a grammar school place in the selection test at 11 was not the irretrievable misfortune which it seemed at the time.

In the larger towns, or populous counties well served by transport, a number of secondary modern schools will sometimes federate to provide alternative fields of study; these are undertaken by the abler pupils normally at the completion of their four-year course. Thus pupils of 15 who a few years ago might have been thankfully gathering up their accumulated school possessions preparatory to leaving are now eagerly applying, with their parents' backing, for permission to enter advanced courses, either at their own school or by transfer to another in federation with it. Such courses which may keep them till they are 17 or even 18 will, in the case of boys, cover, for example, a general preparation for technological occupations, agriculture or horticulture; for girls, hospital training, commercial subjects, art and craft subjects, courses leading to careers in cookery, dressmaking, nursery work or the soft furnishing trades, or even to teaching via the General Certificate of Education taken at 18.

This is not to suggest that the good secondary modern school concentrates on its brightest stream of children while leaving the duller and more backward of its pupils to 'mark time' until they can leave. The lucky school in this regard is that which has on its staff one or more of those teachers who seem to be endowed with special gifts of patience and sympathy which enable them to get *'en rapport'* with children whose mental processes are sluggish. It will be the object of such a teacher to utilise the well-recognised tendency of backward children to prefer to work not as individuals but in a group.

Perhaps such a group will concentrate on some project involving the mastery of some field of study of local or personal interest calculated to keep the curiosity of each child constantly at the highest pitch of which he is capable.

The core of the secondary modern school, however, is, and will always remain, not the backward 12% or 13% or the corresponding percentage in the brighter stream but the remaining 70% to 75% who are ordinary youngsters of average ability. It is these who will probably leave at 15 or 16 to enter minor clerical occupations, to work in shops and canning factories, to go on the land, in due course to drive our buses and operate our telephones. It is these children who make the greatest demand on the teaching staff's infinite capacity for the invention and discovery of new lines of approach and their determination to exact sound standards.

The backbone of any people is the solid mass formed by those categories who do the job near at hand and put into it the very best of which they are capable.

Whatever the approach—and it may be through 'Projects' or schemes of topical interest or concentration on a wide range of practical activities such as those surrounding a 'Young Farmers' Club'—it is likely to be very far from the compulsory gritting of the teeth on the hard subjects of the formal curriculum which their parents experienced in their schooldays. Nevertheless, and this is the essential point, every such project succeeds in introducing, though in a much more stimulating form, just those same subjects, calculations, measuring, drawing, elementary science, English and so on. It is not the field of knowledge to be covered that has changed but the ways by which pupils are led through rather than driven over that field. As the Ministry of Education pamphlet on 'The New Secondary Education' puts it:

> 'The collection and collation of facts, the correlation of sources of knowledge, the interpretation of evidence, the establishment of principles from particular examples, the analysis and synthesis involved, the realisation that the requirements of an investigation demand at some stage the mastery of a technique before further progress can be made—

all these are first-rate training; and the fact that heterogeneous material is being used rather than the more homogeneous material of a particular subject is an advantage rather than a disadvantage.'

There is unfortunately another side to the picture.

There is no doubt that many hundreds of secondary modern school staffs up and down the country have during the past 15 years and with the support of their Local Education Authorities met the challenge with such devotion and daring that their schools have been completely transformed from the senior elementary schools which occupied their buildings before the Act of 1944.

Indeed Professor H. C. Dent, whose book on Secondary Modern Schools published in 1958 should be read by everyone concerned with public education, calculated as a result of visits to hundreds of schools up and down the country and questionnaires to Chief Education Officers that by 1956—

> 16% of schools were carrying out good original work
> 36% sound work showing touches of originality
> 43% sound but unremarkable work
> and only 5% had not moved far beyond the standards of the pre-war senior elementary school.

Anyone, however, who seeks to draw a general picture of the present state of *all* secondary modern schools solely from what he can read in books or in the educational press must be on his guard lest he forms in his mind too rosy a picture. To see children as they really were in the period from 1870 to 1900, it is essential to examine with almost microscopic care, and an informed mind, hundreds of old photographs which have survived from those days. The flesh-and-blood children of the photographs do not look in the least like the idealised children in the oil paintings of that period or those in the illustrations in, for example, *Punch* or the *Illustrated London News*. So it still is with far too many of the Secondary Modern Schools still to be found up and down the country housed in old, badly arranged and cramped buildings; with lavatories as 'gothic' as their architecture; with continually

THE SECONDARY STAGE OF EDUCATION

changing staffs and classes so large that the task of drawing a lively response from each child rather than having to impose education upon him becomes almost impossible.

Nor should the importance of the home background from which the children come be forgotten. A child still spends no more than an eighth of his life from 5 to 15 at school, the other seven-eighths in his home. If the parents are feckless, overindulgent, prepared to accept low standards of morals or manners, slovenly in their speech, more concerned to excuse a lie than condemn it, constantly exposing the child to insecurity or causing him to witness disloyalty or bickering in the home circle they are expecting a miracle—albeit one which sometimes occurs—if they imagine that the school can successfully counteract such influences. Such unhappily circumstanced children have been aptly described as having to make their way through their school life like 'Pit ponies in blinkers'.

Before Hitler's war, an annual examination for 'scholarships' at the grammar school creamed off about 10% or at most 15% of children at the age of 11 and left all the rest to go into the senior elementary schools from which a comparatively small number would pass into junior technical, commercial or art schools at 13.

The first 15 years since the Education Act of 1944 came into force have seen this comparatively simple pattern rearranging itself so that the resulting kaleidoscope is already difficult to depict and is likely to become more and more complex as the century progresses.

The short-term forces at work have been firstly the deeply felt anxiety among parents—themselves the product of the third generation of universal public education—about the reliability of any examination test taken so early as 10, and its capacity to arrive at a just assessment of their child's ability and natural bents so early in his life. Secondly there has been a tendency for the proportion of the 11-year age group admitted to grammar schools to rise from 10% to 25%, 30% or even 50% in some areas so long as the decline of births in the war years kept each annual age group coming forward down to drought level. A third factor has been the determination of the former junior technical schools—which have now become secondary technical schools—to lower their age of entry from 13 to 11 in the hope of getting a better share of the cream.

It is not, unfortunately, necessary to look beyond the early 1960's to see that tens of thousands of children who entered school at five as members of the greatly swollen post-war age groups will be denied the place in a secondary grammar school which their abilities would have earned for them without question if they had reached their eleventh birthday in the late 1940's. Whereas the chance of Tommy or Carol doing well in the common entrance test is already today one of the first topics of conversation between their fathers when they meet in the train and their mothers at any suburban tea-party, these anxieties and dissatisfactions may well have developed by the middle 1960's into a major political issue. An even more serious prospect is that the whole educational atmosphere of the upper forms of the Junior Schools, already tense enough today in some schools as the date of the common entrance test approaches, may be completely warped by the shrinkage of grammar school places in proportion to the much larger number of candidates for them and the inexorable pressure exerted by parents on their children and school staffs.

Some of these pressures may in the long run be relieved, temporarily at least, if the birth-rate declines once more, to that of the pre-war years and the numbers in the schools fall correspondingly. At the time of writing (1959), however, there is little sign of this happening. There are long-term forces at work, too. For it should never be forgotten that class barriers and social stratification have been crumbling away at an ever-increasing pace over the past fifty years before the rising tide of educational opportunity. To the Victorian the rigidities of late 19th-century social stratification must have appeared almost as something ordained by providence. The Victorian elementary school was a waiting-room—very much 'third class' for life. Today, we tend to assume—perhaps too readily when we see the children of the Vicar and our young journalist neighbour passing on their way to the local infants school—that we have left such things behind. The tide is washing over such barriers as remain and they are only intermittently visible. How will even these residual barriers appear, however, to the men and women of the 1970's? Will not our present willingness to tolerate or turn a blind eye to our continued failure to accord complete parity of esteem and treatment to all pupils of secondary school age be viewed in much the same light as we today regard the opacities of the Board School era? It is barely 35 years since a speaker in the House of Commons, who had been Parliamentary Secretary to the Board of Education, in arguing against the raising of the school-leaving age claimed that the cotton industry could never do without the pliant and nimble fingers of the 14-year-old worker. It is less than 25 years since members of the Finance Committees of local authorities would be found bitterly opposing the installation of hot water in new schools as calculated to give children ideas 'above their station'. The young men and women who dared to fight such policies are now middle aged, but some of them are wise enough to realise that the young are always right in the end, if only because they eventually have the last word.

Those who commission and design a school today must think in terms of it lasting 40 to 60 years. Anyone, therefore, who studies the unfolding inter-relationship between the expansion of public education and social change and looks ahead as the country sets about replacing the whole of its first generation of school buildings must ask himself if there is not some way of emancipating the junior schools for their proper task; assuring parents that their children will be able to get into a school which will enable them to reach the highest development of which each is capable; and carrying forward to University and Higher Technological courses every atom of trainable ability which the nation so greatly needs.

A number of highly ingenious solutions have been propounded. All are likely to be the subject of extensive experiment. None is likely to gain universal acceptance but all will inevitably tend to break down our present three-tier secondary school structure within the next 30 years.

First in importance is the experiment of dispensing with any but a purely 'diagnostic' as opposed to a 'competitive' common entrance examination at the end of the junior school course;

admitting all junior school leavers from the whole area to a single large 'comprehensive' school; and organising within that school all the courses which would be found today in a grammar, a secondary technical and a secondary modern school. Such a school, it is claimed, will set the junior schools free to work out their own curricula in terms of activity and experience without any thought of a final competitive examination. It will meet the criticism that parents attach mistaken values to one type of school or the other instead of appreciating that the best school for their particular child is that which can provide the courses of study best suited to his aptitudes and ability. It can do much to make sure that no child of high intelligence, or possessing some highly developed flair for a particular group of studies, falls by the wayside through getting into the wrong stream at 11 or through the poverty of his home background.

In the organisation of such schools, Local Education Authorities are able to draw upon the great body of experience amassed in the United States and Canada. But they have started on this side of the Atlantic with one great advantage. In the comprehensive schools of the United States the social ideal of parity of treatment preceded in point of time instead of following, as it has in England, the general acceptance of the fact that no two children are born equal intellectually; and that to get the best out of a comprehensive school the children must take their place in the form, set or class structure of the school according to their ability and not their age or the initial letter of their surnames. To English eyes, and those of many wise American educationists, one of the most unfortunate results of this historical accident in the U.S. has been to render representation of the school on, for example, the sports field a criterion of excellence more important in the estimation of the pupils than excellence in school work or leadership, and to render the development of what we think of as 'sixth-form' work very rare indeed.

Those who hope to see a rapid expansion of the 'comprehensive' school in England hope and believe that they will be able to preserve the distinctive essences of each present type of secondary school while combining the virtues and carrying the educational potential of each to a higher power. Most of them admit, however, that a school of 1,500 to 2,000 pupils is about the smallest unit in which a satisfactory range of sixth-form work could be economically developed unless and until it becomes the practice for a substantial proportion of the pupils to stay on for at least a five- or six-year course. Schools of smaller size would postulate the 'creaming off' of sixth-form pupils into a central college, or transfer of individuals to federated schools. Within a school of this size, they are confident that wider and more varied courses of studies can be offered to children of every range of ability, together with better laboratories, practical rooms, playing fields, and a wider range of school societies, clubs, and extra curricular activities, such as camping and continental journeys.

The idea has not only won its adherents from among planners and thinkers who, for the reasons set out above, regard it as politically and socially inevitable but among those who have been concerned in the experiments already made.

On the other hand, opposition to it, equally disinterested, has been prolonged and pointed. This opposition has derived principally from the long-standing tradition in English education that a school should never be so large as to prevent the Head knowing every pupil; the staff developing into a closely knit team; and the pupils developing a truer community spirit through a sense of corporate unity. Additionally, it is argued that so long as comprehensive schools are not the sole option offered by the accessible school provision available in any given area the ablest boys and girls will still leach away to secondary schools outside the national system or those which are financially independent of the Local Education Authority. Moreover, they argue, the least able boys and girls who now enjoy opportunities to excel and to achieve leadership in the secondary modern schools will be deprived of these advantages if they are continuously outclassed by those far brighter than themselves in the ' "A" stream' of a comprehensive school. For 'in a working-man's club the University man can always make himself King'.

Unfortunately, the whole discussion of comprehensive schools tended in the early stages—and before a sufficient number had been established to allow a fair test of the conflicting theories—to become super-charged with 'Political Plutonium'. There seemed indeed, at one time, to be a real danger that the interplay of argument and counter argument would obscure the inexorable movement of social forces which had created the original demand for a radical review of the tripartite organisation, a movement which was bound to become more and more pronounced by the early 1960's.

Fortunately wiser counsels now seem to be gaining ground. Former opponents are generous in their recognition of the success of those comprehensive schools which have been established and are prepared to welcome widespead experiment with the comprehensive principle in other suitable areas. Former protagonists for a uniform system of comprehensive schools as the sole goal and organisational panacea now appear prepared to admit other types of organisation so long as they embody an element of the comprehensive principle.

In this the undoubted successes registered by the 50 schools which have, up to the present (1959), been established for a period long enough to afford an objective, though interim, assessment have played an important part.

Sensible delegation of responsibilities from Heads either to housemasters and housemistresses or, as an alternative, to teachers in charge of each yearly entry has been a feature in every school. In most of them further delegation has been arranged to house tutors responsible for smaller groups in each house. Rigid 'form' structures have been broken down into 'setting' to enable children to work at their optimum rate in each subject. Responsibilities and chances of leadership have been distributed widely to children of all ages over the whole range of societies, clubs, games and other activities not forgetting the production of excellent school magazines. Close contacts have been established with local industries on the one hand and with Principals of Technical Institutions on the other. Advice on courses to be taken by individual children is correlated with the careers advice of selected members of the staff and the talks and interviews given by the Youth Employment Service.

In schools of this size, with so many staff to call upon, effective remedial work can be undertaken for the minority groups of retarded or dull children. The retarded are those who may possess average or even superior intelligence but seem unable to measure up to academic work of a commensurate standard; the dull those who are markedly below the average in intelligence. These two groups are usually roughly equal in numbers and may account for 20% to 25% of the annual intake. Few parents can be expected, perhaps, to recognise that their retarded child has made three years' progress in reading in two years but it is unlikely that they will fail to notice how much happier he seems as a result of finding himself someone who matters in a class of 20–30 where before he was always 40th out of 40! The parents themselves, too, have wherever possible been brought into the life of the school through a parent teacher association or by being persuaded to enrol for one of the evening institute activities organised in the school building. Perhaps it is due to such visible demonstrations that their children are now in a school which is 'Plus a little something some others haven't got', as the petrol advertisements used to say, that 80% of the parents are keeping their children on at school after the statutory leaving age in some of the earliest established comprehensive schools.

It is to be hoped that after having had to endure the floodlights for so long the 50 schools, and the many more now projected, will from now on be allowed to burgeon in peace. For the literature which has grown up around them is so vast that it can be truthfully said that never in the history of human education has so much been written by so many about so few!

The development of comprehensive schools has suited those areas which, as in London and Coventry, found it convenient to make something like a clean sweep of their first generation ex-senior elementary school buildings after war-time bombing and post-war improvisations had rendered much of their school plant obsolescent; areas where, as in Anglesey and the Isle of Man, secondary schools had to replace first-generation all-age schools; and areas or parts of areas where new housing estates afforded an opportunity to plan in a virgin field.

An extremely interesting alternative which has commended itself elsewhere, particularly where a well-found network of newly built schools is already in being, is that pioneered in several parts of Leicestershire. It has been described as 'two-tier' secondary organisation. Under this plan selection at eleven is abolished and all children (other than a few 'flyers' of very high calibre who can still proceed straight to the grammar schools) pass from the junior schools into 'High Schools' from 11 to 13 or 14. At this age any child after completing the first three years of the High School course can pass on into a 'second-tier' grammar school. His parents must however be prepared to give an undertaking (unenforceable at law) to keep him there at least till he reaches the age of 16. These grammar schools which form the second tier must, as a corollary, be prepared to organise special courses of a technical or semi-vocational type for those pupils for whom the traditional disciplines of a grammar school education are not appropriate.

This experiment appears to present a number of advantages. It should free the primary schools from the shadow of the 11 plus examination with the pressures and the drills to which that shadow can give rise. It may enhance parental regard for the former secondary modern schools and the former grammar schools alike. It will preserve a system of schools of manageable size. Whether the 'creaming off' of children adjudged to be flyers (so early as 10 plus), to prevent the grammar schools' normal intake being cut off at source too abruptly, will be preserved as a permanent feature of the scheme remains to be seen. The 'first-tier' High Schools too will have to meet two challenges. They will have to widen their courses to embrace the initial stages of G.C.E. studies with the inclusion of modern languages and perhaps Latin. They will also have to solve many problems of leadership and significant courses for those who do not opt for the grammar schools, because they want to leave at 15 or by the end of their fourth year.

The scheme certainly seems to have made a promising beginning in Leicestershire where, in the surburban part of the area selected for its initiation, the 'second round' showed 50% of the 14-year-olds in the grammar schools and in the industrial part 40%. Clearly it will be watched intently by those areas ranging from Carlisle in the north to Stoke-on-Trent, Rotherham and parts of Derbyshire in the Midlands where it may come to be seen as the only way in which many of the advantages of comprehensive education can be achieved without years of delay.

Short of this Leicestershire plan or the completely 'comprehensive' school organised under its single Head and single roof into an expanding series of groupings, 'set', form, house-tutors' group, housemaster's house, lower school, upper school and so on, experiment is likely to be made with 'federation' of Secondary Grammar, Secondary Technical and Secondary Modern schools or of the first two or the second and third. Each will, under such a federation, remain under separate Heads but all (or each pair) will occupy the same 'base' and be fused into one comprehensive whole for games, school clubs, societies and extra curricular activities. Although all the pupils will no doubt wear the same school uniform, it remains to be seen how successfully the respective staffs will be able to cope with the centripedal crowd psychology of the adolescent boy or girl where the crowds are organised in separate schools. The superiorities and disharmonies which have all too often developed between, for example, the 'Classical' and 'Modern' sides in the large boarding 'Public' Schools or even sometimes between 'houses' in the large girls' boarding-schools, seem to point a serious warning.

As Dr. Robin Pedley, Senior Lecturer in Education for the University of Leicester, said in his address to the education section of the British Association at York in September 1959: 'After 15 years of country-wide trial, and support by the most eminent and influential authorities, the system of directing children at the age of eleven into separate types of school is assailed on all sides and indeed (in my view) is on the point of collapse.' Although there still remains a substantial body of educational opinion which would not go all the way with him in this uncompromising view it is indeed becoming more difficult with every year to see what possible device can effect a permanent sealing of the cracks in the present tripartite mould. For the cement used if sealing is to be attempted must be sufficient to withstand the fires of social controversy which already surround it and will increase with the restriction now taking place in the proportion of Secondary Grammar School places to candidates for them. Moreover, the mould itself is likely to appear more and more of an anachronism to each successive generation of parents.

The ordinary citizen faced with a long period of medical treatment, perhaps involving several operations, may sigh for the cosy atmosphere of the small cottage hospital he knew in his youth, but he does not refuse to enter the big Regional Hospital of today, with its many specialist departments, merely on the ground that it seems more impersonal. As with the National Health Service so with the national service of education. Both are increasingly today expected to discharge the function of being an instrument to be used by society for its own improvement in accordance with the dominant social philosophy.

While the '11 plus' fanned by the popular press has been becoming a burning question for the mass of English parents another question which may be described as that of the '18 plus' has begun increasingly to exercise the minds of many leaders of educational thought. A brief statement of the major changes which have come over the university scene since the war will illustrate one facet of this question. Another facet—that concerned with the development of Technological courses parallel to and of equivalent standard to University honours degree courses—will be dealt with in the next chapter. Yet a third aspect concerns the expansion of the facilities for the training of teachers.

Undoubtedly the principal factor underlying the remarkable expansion which has taken place in the Universities has been the growing appreciation in informed quarters of a view which found expression in the University Grants Committee's Report of 1953. This was that a continued increase in expenditure on university education would in the long term be found to be in the national interest, not only because the dependence of this country on manufactured exports made it essential for it to keep in the forefront of scientific and technological development, but more generally because its success in solving its internal problems and maintaining its position of responsibility in world affairs was inseparably bound up with its standards of higher education.

The extent of the expansion can best be illustrated by a table showing the full-time students enrolled in the universities of England, Wales and Scotland in the year before the war, the

THE SECONDARY STAGE OF EDUCATION 61

year 1951–52 when the post-war influx caused by the Government's further education and training scheme for 45,000 men and women who had been in the Services had nearly worked itself out, 1957–58—the last year for which complete figures are available, and October 1959 for which no more than the totals are yet available.

FULL-TIME STUDENTS ENROLLED IN THE UNIVERSITIES OF ENGLAND, SCOTLAND AND WALES

1938–39		1951–52		1957–58		October 1959
Men	Women	Men	Women	Men	Women	Men and Women
38,557	11,689	63,970	19,488	71,855	23,587	
50,246		83,458		95,442		100,000

The University Grants Committee have expressed the view that the increase in demand indicated by these figures will carry the number to 124,000 students by the mid 1960's; that there is a possibility of a further increase of about 10% (i.e., to 136,000) in the late 1960's; that two-thirds of this expansion to 124,000 will be in students of science and technology who will then number 55,000, or 86% more than they numbered in 1955–56; and that a substantial though smaller rise will take place in those studying the humanities and social science, carrying them to 49,000, an increase of 34%.

The Grants Committee are also reasonably confident that these increases, if achieved, together with those which will result from developments at Colleges of Advanced Technology in England and Wales and at Central Institutions in Scotland, should produce the growth in the number of qualified scientists and technologists which the Scientific Man Power Committee of the Advisory Council on Scientific Policy have estimated to be required; that the amounts of non-recurrent and recurrent grants to which they have been authorised to commit the Treasury in respect of the capital cost of buildings, administration, salaries, maintenance, repairs and other expenditure, will be adequate to meet the greatly increased volume of new building which will be required as well as the increase in staffs to avoid the lowering of standards; and that students' choices will continue, as in the past, to show themselves to be sufficiently sensitive to respective demand to secure the proportionate increases aimed at in different Faculties.*

As an illustration it may be mentioned that the limits on grant commitment on buildings started in the current year (1959) is 12 million, and this will rise to 15 million each year from 1960 to 1963. These sums are exclusive of the cost of sites, fees and equipment and do not cover the cost of the Imperial College expansion. As regards current expenditure the grants promised for the new Quinquennian rise from 30·6 million for the year 1957–58 to 39·5 million for the year 1961–62, excluding in each case the cost of the new rates of salary for academic staff which took effect in 1957.

Trends which emerge from any study of university development since the war are that:

(a) The number of pupils remaining at school to the age of 17 and over (77,000 in 1958) is more than twice as great as before the war.

(b) The number of passes at advanced level in the General Certificate of Education increased in each of the seven years 1951–58 and much the largest increase took place in the last three years of the period. The total increase over this period was 57·7%. The increase in mathematics and physics were 109·5% and 78·5% respectively. These figures may, however, to some extent, over-state the real increase as there is some tendency for individuals to take more subjects and also to take the examination in successive years.

(c) In the light of this rising tide in secondary school sixth forms the number of applications for admission received by universities has increased far more than the capacity of the university departments. For example, in October 1955 31,000 applicants submitted 70,000 applications for 18,000 places at different universities (Oxford, Cambridge and Aberdeen excepted). Unfortunately no solution has yet been found which promises to reduce this duplication. It is in itself, of course, a symptom of greater competition for entry since few candidates can be certain of acceptance at the university of their first choice.

THE SECONDARY STAGE OF EDUCATION

(d) The shift in social background, as measured by parents' occupations, has been more marked than the shift from the background of fee-paying to that of non-fee-paying schools. Nevertheless the University Grants Committee have expressed the opinion that there can be little doubt that in recent years an increased proportion of university entrants have come from families in which they are the first generation to receive a university education.

(e) Correspondingly the proportion of students holding scholarships, exhibitions or other awards, whether from public or private funds providing wholly or in part for the payment of their fees or other expenses, has risen substantially from 41·1% in 1938–39 to 72·8% in 1949–50 and 79·2% in 1957–58. This still, however, left a total of about 20,000 students occupying places at the universities who reached the universities without assistance.

(f) The five or six main streams of students which formed the total entry of 27,676 in October 1957 could probably be analysed as follows (completely accurate figures are not available since it is not known precisely into which categories some 3,800 students entering Scottish Universities would fall):

(i) Supplemental State Scholarships (England and Wales), i.e., awards offered to holders of 'open' university awards to place them on the same financial footing as State scholars   1,602

(ii) State Scholarships (England and Wales):
    Awarded on G.C.E. 1,972
    State studentships 243
    Scholarships for mature students 30
                                                                        2,245

(iii) Major awards made to universities by L.E.A.'s and taken up   15,222

(iv) Students reaching the universities without assistance .. .. say 6,000

(v) Students coming from homes outside the United Kingdom .. .. say 2,500

Thus access to University education today would appear to be in much the same case as was access to secondary education from 1931 to 1944 before secondary school fees were abolished. Parents who were ready to pay the school fee without question could usually secure the admission of their child, if he was of reasonable intelligence; and he would thereafter enjoy the concealed subvention of any endowments the school possessed and any grant made available by the Ministry or Local Education Authority. The parent whose child reached the school by the scholarship ladder on the other hand had to pay the fee, a reduced fee, or nothing according to his annual income.

(g) The increase in cost of university education and the small proportion of it now borne by fees, endowments, grants from local authorities and donations is well illustrated by the following table:

	1951–52		1957–58		Increase Per cent
	Amount £m	Per cent	Amount £m	Per cent	
Parliamentary Grants	17,127	66·5	34,953	70·7	104·02
Fees	3,807	14·8	5,702	11·5	49·7
Endowments	1,348	5·2	1,757	3·6	30·3
Grants from local authorities	1,044	4·1	1,402	2·8	34·2
Donations and subscriptions	485	1·9	520	1·1	7·2
Other income	1,937	7·5	2,027 *		
Total	25,748	100·0	41,595	100·0	61·5

* In addition £3,008,898 was received in Payments for Research.

The scope of the contribution which the universities now make to research, and to national life at a hundred different points, is so extensive and so well recognised that no one would be so naïve as to suggest that on a simple division sum the figures in the table above mean that as against an average fee of £60 the university student of 1957–58 was enjoying an annual concealed subvention from parliamentary funds of £366 plus annual subsidies of £18 from endowments, £15 from subventions to the universities by Local Authorities and £5 from donations and subscriptions; and that on top of these concealed subventions he may well be receiving maintenance from the Ministry of Education or his Local Education Authority, ranging up to a maximum of the full university fees, plus £325 a year. (It is perhaps worth noting that a similar concealed subvention exists in the case of teachers' training colleges. There however the recognised student never pays more than the £50 tuition fee whereas the private student must pay the full cost of the order of £250.)

Nevertheless, figures of this order do render it invidious to have to admit that there is, at present, no clear answer which can be given to a question which is likely to be asked with ever-increasing insistence as both direct and indirect costs of university education and pressure for admission rise. This question is: can any firm assurance be given that every one of the 6,000 applicants annually who still appear to obtain admission unsponsored by the State or the Local Authorities, but solely through the willingness of their parents to meet their fees and maintenance, are at least as fully capable of profiting by the University course as those who have obtained 'open' awards from the University, State scholarships from the Ministry or Major County Awards from Local Education Authorities?

If no such firm assurance is forthcoming it is inevitable that the suggestion will arise that many among the 6,000 will have been accepted in preference to other, and possibly academically better, candidates because their fathers could 'pull a string' as old members of the college—or even because of some special prowess on the field of sport. Inevitably too it can be suggested that a large proportion would be found among those who eventually leave the university without gaining a degree.

Unfortunately the percentage of students who do find themselves in this position at the end of their first or second year and, to a lesser extent, at the end of their full university course, is by no means negligible. True the proportion of outstandingly good and outstandingly weak students is lower and that of good second-class students higher than it was before the war.

Nevertheless an inquiry into the records of 15,256 students admitted in October 1952 to courses of three or four years in Arts, pure science and technology, showed that no more than 80·6% were successful by the end of the session 1955–56. Of the other 19·4%, 2·7% had been readmitted to continue their courses in October 1956. Of the 16·7% who had left the universities without success, 5·4% left for reasons other than academic failure, without completing their courses. The proportion who had failed academically was thus 11·3%. This result was not inconsistent with smaller inquiries conducted at Liverpool and University College, London.

A detailed analysis of the 6,000 would probably reveal that the great majority of them had been offered a place as a result of their performances in the competition for college 'open' awards but had been unable to apply for a State scholarship or Major County Award owing to their parents' income. Nevertheless it remains a question to which those who cannot secure a place in the University are clearly entitled to a satisfactory answer.

Has the time come, then, for the universities, while preserving freedom of selection and rejection in the matter of the candidates they ultimately admit, to follow the pattern accepted by grant-aided secondary schools when secondary education became free in 1944? This would imply that every candidate should first be sponsored (either for remission of the university fee or for completely free tuition and maintenance during the university terms.) The sponsoring bodies would be the universities themselves for winners of 'open' university scholarships and exhibitions; the Ministry for State scholarship winners; the local education authorities for those candidates qualified under the rules laid down in their approved schemes of aid; and no doubt the Commonwealth Relations Office and Foreign Office.

As to whether tuition fees alone should be abolished or completely free tuition and maintenance should be instituted there are two schools of thought:

(*i*) The first and most uncompromising would argue that the present annual entry from England and Wales to the universities allows only just over four individuals (4·1) out of every 100 in the age group to secure a place and that even if university figures rise to 124,000 by the mid nineteen sixties, this 4·1% will barely increase because the age group will then be 50% larger. Accordingly, having regard to the concealed subvention which is made available to every winner of a university place, and the imperative necessity of making the best use of every such place to cultivate to their maximum potential the gifts of the cream of each age group, no student should be admitted unless sponsored by a college as the winner or near winner of a university 'open' award, the State as the winner of a State scholarship, or the L.E.A. as reaching a level of achievement prescribed in its scheme of aid; and that every such applicant should thereupon be afforded remission of fees plus full maintenance irrespective of parental means. Those who support this view tend to point out that the concealed subvention is likely to be in every case many times as large as the fees; that any parent, however substantial his means, can claim, with justice, that he pays for his children's education (and often a proportion of that of many other children too) by the rates and taxes he pays over the term of his life; that he should not therefore be taxed separately because his child is clever enough to secure a university place; that the Armed Forces have already abolished their means test at Sandhurst and other training establishments; and that it is illogical to offer free secondary education to all without taking the next step and offering free university education to all those who prove themselves capable of securing one of the four places available to every hundred in their age group.

This appears to be a view which is gaining ground in certain industrial circles, as witness the number of scholarship schemes, e.g., the Trevelyan Scholarships, which now offer a university education without parental contribution.

(*ii*) A second body of opinion, while accepting the proposition that university places are now too valuable and too competitive to allow them to be purchased for unsponsored students at a fraction of their real cost, argues that there seems no sufficient reason why parents should not continue to pay according to their means for the food, clothing and living expenses of their sons and daughters while they are enjoying such privileges at the expense of the taxpayer, the pious founder and the local ratepayer. To relieve all parents altogether of such charges might indeed, it is suggested, enable the wealthier parents to make personal allowances to their sons and daughters while at the University. This could only have the effect of accentuating distinctions between individual members of the student body which it has been the object of past policy to diminish.

The institution of admission 'by sponsorship only' to every university place would involve the payment or remission by the sponsor (College, Ministry or Local Education Authority) of the university fee in every case but the assessment of the parent for the standard figure of maintenance.

Those who advocate this middle course can point to the similar pattern which operates in the case of maintenance allowances where hardship exists for secondary school pupils who continue to receive full-time education after the age of 15. It is argued however, by the 'full remission' school of thought, that it is more reasonable for the community to expect a parent to feed, clothe and house his child while at school, only paying a maintenance allowance to represent the extra cost of keeping him in attendance, than to expect the parent to continue to do so when the child has become an adult receiving an expensive course of training, often away from home, in order to fit him to use his talents in a job of national importance. This has undoubtedly been the consideration underlying the existing and comparatively generous standard figure of maintenance and parental income scales.

If public opinion should ever reach the point of demanding that all places at the University should be restricted solely to those students who are sponsored by a university or college (as the winner or near winner of an 'open' college scholarship), the Ministry (as the winner of a state scholarship), a Local Authority (as the recipient of a county major award after acceptance by a university) it would be logical to provide that:

(*i*) all winners of 'open' scholarships should be allowed to retain the value of that scholarship, plus supplementation to the level of the state scholarship, including the £50 annual honorarium paid by the Ministry to state scholarship winners whose parental means do not entitle them to anything more

(*ii*) all winners of state scholarships should receive the £50 honorarium in addition to remission of fees

(*iii*) all recipients of county major awards from Local Education Authorities should receive remission of fees, plus maintenance according to their parents' means

and that

(*iv*) all those charitable funds at present used by schools to provide leaving scholarships to the university should be devoted to leavers entering upon non-university courses or, perhaps better still, to preventing the loss to the universities of brilliant pupils who would leave their secondary schools prematurely owing to the economic position of their parents.

Such a system would provide a sensible graduation of awards to meet one of the commonest points made by headmasters and experienced sixth-form masters in any private discussion of the present basis of awards. This is that they too often today encounter boys who in the past would have worked unremittingly to obtain an 'open' scholarship or exhibition, or at least a state scholarship, but today do not seem to be putting the last ounce of effort into their work because they know that failing an 'open' award or State scholarship, they can be reasonably sure of a County Major Award of the same value. So long as there is no differentiation in value between the three types of award, the argument that the first two carry an academic kudos, which may make all the difference in securing a place on a short list for promotion at the age of 30, is not inclined to impress any but the rather exceptional young man or woman of 17 or 18!

It is such questions as these that are at present under review by a departmental committee appointed by the Ministry of Education under the chairmanship of Sir Colin Anderson, and the answers will no doubt be made public almost before this book appears.

---

*p. 41: As the Crowther report shows (page 231, Table 35), the number of boys and girls in sixth forms has been increased by 5% per annum for the past ten years and by 1968 there may well be 213 boys and girls for every 100 today.

*p. 62: The view is now gaining ground that the universities will have to increase their number of students to 180,000 by the late 1960's.

III

TECHNOLOGICAL AND FURTHER EDUCATION

THE WIDE SCOPE OF TECHNOLOGICAL AND FURTHER EDUCATION. THE MAIN CATEGORIES OF STUDENT. THE IMPORTANCE OF DAY-TIME RELEASE. NATIONAL CERTIFICATE COURSES. IS OUR HIGHER TECHNOLOGICAL EDUCATION FACING UP TO THE CHALLENGE OF THE NEW INDUSTRIAL REVOLUTION? IS A SUFFICIENT PLACE ALLOTTED TO THE HUMANITIES? PROGRESS SINCE THE END OF THE WAR. IS 'EDUCATION FOR LEISURE' OUT OF DATE? THE IMPORTANCE OF ADULT EDUCATION.

'CALL things by their right names and do not confuse together things which are essentially different. A thorough knowledge of one science, and a superficial acquaintance with many, are not the same thing; a smattering of a hundred things, or a memory for detail, is not a philosophical or comprehensive view. Recreations are not education; accomplishments are not education. Do not say the people must be educated when after all you only mean amused, refreshed, soothed, put into good spirits and good humour, or kept from vicious excesses. I do not say that such amusements are not a great gain, but they are not education. Education is a high word; it is the preparation for knowledge, and it is the imparting of knowledge in proportion to that preparation.'

It is amusing to speculate whether any friend of Cardinal Newman who read his *Scope and Nature of University Education* on its publication in 1859 was hardy enough to ask him what his reactions would be if he were to return a century later to find that the number of men and women attending English Universities standing side by side would reach from his beloved Oxford to Hyde Park Corner; those attending full-time and part-time day courses in Major Establishments for Further Education and Art would cover the 57 miles four deep; and that the column would become more than 20 deep if those attending evening classes were also added.

He might, quite legitimately and consistently, reply: 'Show me first what each individual man, woman or child in this respectable army of 2,273,777 [1958] students is doing. What is the motive of each? How far is each in serious pursuit of seasoned knowledge? What in sum do the total hours they spend in their classes or homework amount to when compared with those worked in a year by the schoolboy or University undergraduate? What in sum are they contributing to the nation's life or livelihood?'

Such a challenge would, in fact, illustrate the extraordinary difficulties which beset anyone who essays to give a short, balanced but still readable account of the present state of 'Technological and Further Education' in Britain. For under the comprehensive umbrella of these four words, 'Technological and Further Education', one will find the student at work before an electron microscope or helping to find a solution to some problem in nuclear physics referred to the research department of a College of Advanced Technology by Harwell; the sea apprentice taking correspondence courses provided by a Local Education Authority for him while he is at sea, or receiving practical training on a seagoing yacht also maintained by the Authority; the rising business manager taking a refresher course in business administration; elderly pigeon fanciers or campanologists raptly discussing the finer points of their respective hobbies; the student of naval architecture in the fifth year of his course for the National Diploma; the young woman from West Africa taking millinery and dressmaking classes on five days a week followed by cake-making and confectionery on each of five evenings, who will explain to an inquirer that she intends on her return to Ghana to open an emporium for the complete clothing and furnishing of weddings, from the dress of the tiniest dusky bridesmaid to the three-tier wedding cake itself; the suburban housewife sitting before a pillow covered with bobbins on which she is working out some intricate pattern in Nottingham lace; the teenager releasing some of her pent-up energy in a ballroom dancing class conducted as an attractive counterweight to a grouped course in commercial subjects; and the student with a rare gift for creative design putting the finishing touches to a silver coffee set or an intricate piece of jewellery.

In March 1958 15,369 full-time teachers and 50,000 part-time teachers were serving in establishments of Technology, schools of art and evening institutes. Yet it is regrettable, though perhaps not altogether surprising, what a small proportion of the educational world or even that of industry and commerce has hitherto treated it as a matter of first-class importance to become better acquainted with our now rapidly expanding system. Those who are middle aged, of course, grew up into a world which died 30 or 40 years ago; a world in which as between the scientist and the rest of mankind there was a great gulf fixed; a world in which prestige, social and academic, was centred in other quarters of the educational field; a world in short which tended to dismiss technical education as something predominantly concerned with livelihood and having little cultural and virtually no religious or moral content. In short their attitude towards the subject was a reflection of that of Thurber to electricity. 'I don't understand Technological Education, and no one must explain it to me!'

Many an 'Arts' graduate whose sense of duty or natural enthusiasm has prompted him to pick up one of the weighty tomes on technological education and has started—as even Arts graduates sometimes do—by flipping over the pages and looking at the pictures first, must have put it sadly down for later perusal with the comment that the avocations of his fellow men and women seem to be inconceivably complicated! For the very first picture probably showed him a group of students studying a 'machine with an unwound salient pole rotor which behaves as a differential when the opposite ends of a stator winding are connected to two polyphase suppliers'.

Probably the simplest simile which the ordinary individual can employ in attempting to get a conspectus of our system of Further Education would be that of one of those East African rivers which rise in a broad but shallow lake, from which much evaporation occurs, and meander slowly at first as a broad stream through flat country. The main stream is joined at intervals by tributary streams but gradually narrows, deepens and quickens as it passes through gorges on its way to the sea. The deepest layers of water always, however, maintain an undertow which makes them seemingly less purposeful than those on the surface.

In such a simile the broad lake would represent the great mass of those who on leaving secondary modern schools at 15 enter at once upon full- or part-time courses in Technical and Art schools or Evening Institutes.

The most easily distinguished of the innumerable small streams of such students which feed the lake would be that composed of young men and women who on leaving school have entered mining, building, one of the manufacturing industries, commerce or one of the occupations (such as grocery or hairdressing) which confer certificates of competence and have been released by their employer to attend classes affording part-time day education.

As the river emerges from the lake, small rivulets of such students continue to join it for some years; in fact nearly one half of the number attending such part-time release classes is composed of young men and women of 18 or over.

At about 16 the river is joined by a purposeful stream of ambitious young men and women intent on obtaining by three years' intensive work in day or evening classes combined with concurrent daytime 'works experience' one of the National Certificates. These are awarded jointly by the Ministry of Education, and one of the many Professional Institutes (such as the Institution of Mechanical Engineers), membership of which may represent a possible apex of their chosen vocation after some years' further training.

The fast-moving upper layer of water in the gorges would represent those taking advanced full-time or part-time scientific or technological courses at University Departments of Technology, Science or Engineering, a College of Advanced Technology, a Regional College or one of the six National Colleges which provide special facilities for advanced studies for industries which, though important to the national economy, are too small to justify provision at more than one centre, e.g., Rubber Technology or Food Technology. Those who follow such courses usually do so with a view to filling administrative posts, originating and directing research, applying the latest discoveries of science to production and with an ultimate eye to the Board Room. A proportion of them will, however, become high-grade technicians rather than technologists.

The slow-moving but deeper layers would represent those who had passed through the phase of carving out a career and building a family. Such students would probably have entered upon a period when they could find time to satisfy a desire to seek some more satisfying philosophy of life in tutorial Adult Education classes.

Shallows and pools by the side of the gorges would be found to be full of those taking craft, literary, artistic, dramatic or home-making courses in satisfaction of their aesthetic interests, their determination to enjoy a higher standard of life on a limited income, or a praiseworthy resolution to make the most profitable use of their leisure time. An encouraging trend in evening institute class entries today is that 15% are those of young women trying to learn for themselves about cooking, sewing and child-rearing.

Let us now go back to the source, examine each of these categories of student, and determine, so far as it is possible to do so, what brings each into being.

It would be wise first, however, to recall two important features which are too often overlooked although they are present virtually throughout the whole of our provision, whether it be in full-time day, part-time day, or in evening classes.

The first is that no one need seek further education after the end of the period of compulsory full-time schooling. The great majority of students in every type of class are there because they have felt a need to equip themselves more satisfactorily for life or for their chosen livelihood. The second is that the work of the teacher becomes much more straightforward once the physiological see-saw between childhood and maturity, which makes the teaching of the adolescent so difficult, has been left behind. Men and women, even quite young men and women, who are no longer 'pupils' regard the tract of knowledge they have themselves elected to cultivate with different and clearer eyes. Anyone who entertains any doubts about the value of an inner urge for self-education might profitably try an experiment. He should spend an hour writing down on one sheet of paper all those things he remembers because at some time he was compelled to master them. On another sheet he should put down all those things he knows because the stimulus to explore that particular field of knowledge came from within himself.

To return to the lake. Substantial efforts are now made to persuade as high a proportion of youngsters as possible to join an evening class, sometimes in their last term at school or more generally in the following September. They are made by the staffs of secondary modern schools, by Youth Employment Officers at the school-leaving interview they arrange with every individual leaver, by employers with a sense of responsibility towards the new entrants to their works or business and by sensible parents. Some are encouraged to work towards the taking of subjects relevant to their chosen vocation in the General Certificate of Education. If they do so they will find themselves more on a level with the stream entering two years later from the secondary technical and secondary grammar schools to enrol for National Certificate Courses.

Others are persuaded to enter upon preliminary craft, technical or commercial courses probably leading to one of the group of examinations conducted by the City and Guilds of London Institute, the Royal Society of Arts or one of the other comparable examining bodies.

Others again can only be persuaded to join an Evening Institute presenting more the appearance of a boys' or girls' club. Here the object of the staff will be to lead them to realise powers, interests and aptitudes hitherto dormant or unsuspected through such pursuits as physical training, games, boxing, home carpentry, hobbies, music and popular science. If pride of achievement can be established, they may be guided through such pursuits into a desire to enter on some course of training of a more formal nature.

It would be interesting to ask a dozen ordinary acquaintances what proportion of the population aged fifteen to twenty they would expect to find still at school or at universities, training colleges for teachers, colleges of technology, commerce or art or attending evening classes. The correct answer will astonish most people:

MEN AND BOYS

Age	Schools*	Universities	Teacher Training Colleges	Technical, Commercial and Art Colleges and Evening Institutes			Total
				Full-time	Part-time day	Evening only	
20		6·1	1·2	1·4	9·4	9·8	27·9
19	0·7	2·9	0·2	1·6	13·6	13·0	32·0
18	4·5	1·3	0·1	1·9	18·1	17·8	43·7
17	11·1			1·9	24·6	23·8	61·4
16	20·0			2·1	24·5	25·3	71·9
15	37·4			2·4	16·2	24·5	80·5

* Includes all grant-aided schools, recognised independent schools and other independent schools.

WOMEN AND GIRLS

Age	Schools	Universities	Teacher Training Colleges	Technical, Commercial and Art Colleges and Evening Institutes			Total
				Full-time	Part-time day	Evening only	
20		2·0	1·8	0·4	0·7	9·5	14·4
19	0·4	1·3	3·6	0·6	1·2	11·2	18·3
18	2·3	0·8	1·3	1·1	2·2	14·9	22·6
17	8·8			2·0	6·0	20·3	37·1
16	18·5			3·5	7·1	23·7	52·8
15	35·7			4·0	5·2	23·1	68·0

The lower percentage of girls is no doubt accounted for by the fact that many girls must help in the home with younger children in the evenings. Preparation for a career outside the home probably does not assume an importance in their lives comparable with that in the case of a boy either in their own eyes or that of their parents, because 85% of them can look forward to marriage before they are 30. Nevertheless, 47% of all girls and women between 15 and 65 in Britain are now in employment and this percentage only falls to 40% after 21.

Heartening though the picture presented by these figures may, at first sight, appear, as a corrective it should not be forgotten

(a) that the school system in the U.S.A., after shedding about 20% of pupils at the ages of 12, 13 and 14, apparently succeeds in keeping 75% of the remaining 80% at the Secondary High Schools up to at least 17. At that stage about 15% pass into skilled and 45% into other occupations. The remaining 40% (i.e. 30% of the total age group) proceed to one of the 131 'private' or 'state' Universities, one of the 694 Liberal Arts Colleges or one of the 529 Junior Colleges (sometimes called Community Colleges).

(b) that in Western Germany virtually the whole school population (after leaving at 14 or 15 according to the 'Land' in which they live) continue their education part-time at Day Continuation Schools (Berufschulen).

The greater number of the high proportion of the boys in the 16 and 17-year-old groups shown in the table above as attending part-time day classes will be students released by their employers, without loss of wages, to take for one full day or two half-days over a 30-week year (145 hours a year on the average) subjects which are usually related to their specific occupations. About a quarter of their number will, however, be found to be studying subjects of a general educational nature.

The name 'Bevin boys' was attached by the Press to young men exempted from military service to serve in the mining industry. Some such soubriquet might well have been applied, however, to the young men and women who now (1958) form the far from negligible army of 434,672 daytime release students. For it was actually Mr. Ernest Bevin who, as Minister of Labour and National Service, at the height of our wartime difficulties in 1942 asked the Employers' Federation and the Trades Union Council to consider the position of young people in Industry with a view to their better training. The report of the Joint Consultative

Committee, which the two bodies set up as the result of Mr. Bevin's initiative, led most Industries to prepare schemes for the recruitment and training of their juveniles and, with the encouragement of the Ministry of Labour, to establish the National Apprenticeship Council and its Regional Councils.

At the present time there are about 80 such schemes in operation. In nearly every one of these an obligation is placed upon the Associated Employers to make provision for part-time release of the young worker. This form of continuative education was held in high regard among the more far-sighted employers in pre-war years. They recognised its direct cash value in the reduction of scrapped work, accidents, and misunderstandings between departments. They insisted in fact that the classes should be kept going even at the height of the war. Nevertheless there were only 41,000 students in such classes in 1939. To have achieved more than a tenfold increase in 20 years, through an alliance between the social conscience and the enlightened self-interest of employers and their controlling grades of staff (not forgetting the foremen), is a fitting sequel to Mr. Bevin's initiative during what was certainly England's darkest albeit her 'finest hour'.

The strictly educational importance of this rising tide cannot be too strongly emphasized.

As we saw in the previous chapter, full-time Secondary Education up to 18, especially when it involves two or more years of sixth-form work, is admirable for the boy whose mind can genuinely be unlocked by it. Something like a law of diminishing returns too often begins to operate in the less academically gifted boy, however, as his mental capacities and his interest in the different subjects of his course reach their ceiling. This is partly because all the school can do for him, so long as he is at school full time, is to provide him with a diet of general principles and seek to fix them in his mind by expecting him to work artificial problems. These artificial problems have to be devised by his teachers and the writers of school text-books to illustrate those general principles. So long as he is in the upper register of the wave-band of academic aptitude and is not approaching his ceiling these artificial problems need not be too complex or abstract for his comprehension. Once he has mastered them they

TECHNOLOGICAL AND FURTHER EDUCATION

merely have to be borne as a burden on his memory. If, on the other hand, he is not in that upper register of the wave-band and is perhaps actually 'bumping on his ceiling' such an academic diet will sooner or later prove too rich for him. The result will be broader and broader patches of partial comprehension and imperfect assimilation with boredom as the inevitable concomitant.

This is not the case, however, where he has put his first foot on the ladder of employment before being forced to travel too far along the road of disillusionment about his ability to keep up with the 'A' stream. If at that point an intelligent employer releases him from the garage, radio shop, or chemist's the same principles which he might find great difficulty in comprehending at once from books and set problems may indeed come to him as comparatively simple links holding together the complex facts he is encountering at work and relieving rather than burdening the memory.

An encouraging feature of the post-war expansion of day release has been the progressive tendency to take advantage of the growing numbers to classify and guide students into the type of work most appropriate to their particular educational antecedents and aptitudes. Thus one will now find classes following a simple curriculum for the plant operative, craft courses for those likely to become skilled craftsmen, high grade courses for technicians and junior supervisory staff and National Certificate courses for those capable of becoming high-grade technicians or future professional staff.

The University Professor, who has reached that eminence by his ability to absorb, analyse, synthesise and build upon the thought of the philosophers and scientists, may in moments of self-deprecation be tempted to wonder whether the highly practical and intelligent young man who comes in to mend his radio might not have been in his shoes had his full-time education not ceased so early. Such musings in nine cases out of ten would probably do more credit to the Professor's heart than to his head. Equally it would be a mistake for him to fail to recognise that the young man probably continued his education to far better purpose by part-time day classes, after the doors of the Secondary Modern School closed behind him, than he would have done by spending a much greater number of hours in full-time studies which were becoming increasingly meaningless or irksome to him. The young man himself would probably put it much more trenchantly, in his own idiom, by saying that he felt during his last term at school as though his mental battery was permanently attached to a trickle charger. When he got into a job and put his battery to work he found that a periodic high amperage recharge at the technical institute seemed to rejuvenate it!

The next distinct and purposeful stream of ambitious young men and women joins English Technical Colleges at about the age of 16 to enter upon 'National Certificate' courses. In the absence of up-to-date statistics it is difficult to determine the exact composition and educational antecedents of this body of students. Sample analyses relating to those attending particular colleges in the north of England suggest that up to half of them probably came from secondary technical schools, and the remaining half came in about equal proportions from the secondary grammar and the secondary modern schools. These north country analyses would probably put the secondary technical proportion too high so far as the country as a whole is concerned. Nevertheless proportionately secondary technical schools have the finest record of any type of school in sending forward their pupils to success in technological education. Those who enter from the secondary grammar schools, where 60% of the sixth forms are now taking science as their main subject, will be those who, after taking the General Certificate of Education at 16, have been recruited into industry. Those who enter from the secondary modern schools will possibly, though not invariably, be those who have either stayed on at school for a fourth or fifth year or, having left at 15, have been working in evening classes at the Technical College in preliminary courses or for the General Certificate of Education. These National Certificate courses generally follow a similar pattern, namely, three years' intensive study in day or evening classes on three or four nights a week, with concurrent workshop experience or office training and, normally, some home study. At the end of the three years an examination is taken for the first award, namely, the National Certificate at 'Ordinary level'. This may be followed by two more years' even more intensive application leading to the

National Certificate at Higher Level. There are, however, variations. For example, a comparatively small though growing number of students obtain a National Diploma in Mechanical, Electrical or Production Engineering, Mining or Building by full-time courses of two or three years' duration. Again, the Higher Certificates in Chemical Engineering and Commerce take three years of part-time study to obtain. Another important common feature is that the teachers who have carried out the actual instruction of the candidates share in the preparation of the examination papers which are 'moderated' subsequently and the scripts assessed by external assessors. This at the inception of the National Certificate Scheme was a distinctively English contribution to examination technique. It is designed to overcome a difficulty, present in all purely external examinations. In such examinations the good candidate may, as Sir Winston Churchill remarked of his examinations at Harrow, be asked all the questions to which he does not know the answer or none of those in which he could excel. The poor candidate may make an exceptionally lucky series of choices in his pre-examination revision. There are now 15 subjects in which National Certificates can be gained. Five are Engineering subjects (Chemical, Civil, Mechanical, Electrical and Production). Four are allied to Chemistry (Chemistry, Applied Chemistry, Applied Physics and Metallurgy). Four represent some of our largest fields of employment (Building, Mining, Commerce and Textiles). Finally, there are certificates in Naval Architecture and Management studies. A sixteenth subject, Retail Distribution, enrolled its first students a few years ago. The number of students taking the examinations each year has multiplied by six (from 5,797 to 35,572) since the year before the war. Rather more than half stay the course and pass at ordinary level. Of those who then proceed to attempt the courses at Higher level about 70% win through. The same kind of subtle, though irrational, distinction which leads the community to confer greater social prestige on doctors than on dentists unfortunately tends in some branches of Industry to be applied to the holder of a University degree vis-à-vis the holder of a National Certificate. Young men who have won through their five years' grind to obtain such a certificate, however, will usually reap a rich reward in their chosen vocation. The young man who does win through, especially when he started from a Secondary Modern School, will have shown a persistence and a willingness to 'scorn delights and live laborious days' just as great as that required of many University degree students at 'Pass' though perhaps hardly at 'Honours' level. What is more, he will have possessed himself of a qualification which is recognised by the knowledgeable and under the Burnham salary scale for teachers of Technological subjects as of degree standard. In any country less governed by tradition the hood and gown would set their seal on his endeavour.

The inquirer who passes on to study the national provision for Technological and Further Education at the highest levels will find that his mind at once becomes preoccupied with a whole series of questions both practical and speculative.

On every side he sees evidence that a new Industrial Revolution is rushing upon the manufacturing nations of the world almost with the speed and urgency of an Atomic chain reaction. The boundaries of science are being daily pushed outwards so rapidly that new sciences seem to come into being overnight. Their very names will be sought in vain in the pre-war text-books—electronics, ultrasonics, linear acceleration, automation, radioactive isotopes, carbon 14 analysis. Every one of them must clearly introduce widespread modifications in the time-honoured techniques and practice of a whole group of Industries and open up an absorbing vista of new industrial applications. The extent to which their development has been matched by improvements in the design of traditional sources of power can be illustrated by noting that a single boiler can today produce 750,000 horse power. This would be sufficient to provide the whole national consumption of electricity in the year 1900. It is not overstating the matter to say that our standard of life may hang on what can be made of our young people by the teacher of science and engineering. For Technology is becoming the modern millstone for our daily bread.

How far are the Government, the Universities and the Local Educational Authorities going out to meet this challenge? Do they display sufficient evidence that they are as keenly alive to it as are the Governments of the U.S.S.R., the U.S.A. and our continental competitors? How far are we producing in the necessary numbers and at the necessary level of quality scientists and technologists capable of administering the large-scale industrial amalgamations which the full development of such new sciences will postulate; men who can originate and direct research; men who can apply the latest discoveries of science to production; men who, in addition to commanding respect as scientists or technologists, have the qualities which will lead to the Board Room? How far are we training the engineer scientists and development engineers, the design, manufacture, operative and sales managers? Are the British public still perhaps tending too readily to think that the function of Technological Colleges is to train technical assistants, designer draughtsmen, foremen and craftsmen, and that the training of the scientists and administrators can safely be left to the Universities? Ought we not, as the price of our very survival, to set ourselves, and achieve with a real sense of urgency, a new goal, the appropriate training of the whole manpower of the nation? Ought not scientific education at the highest levels to be shared equitably between the University Departments of Science and Engineering, Colleges of Advanced Technology and a limited number of top-level Regional Colleges? Ought we not to pay far more regard than hitherto to the production of Technologists, scientists and technicians for the Commonwealth and to facilitating the interchange of those we produce with those trained in the Universities of the Dominions?

Or again, how far dare we view with any degree of complacency our provision for the admixture of liberal and humanistic with scientific studies? Are we doing enough to satisfy the craving for a more satisfactory philosophy of life which should, perhaps at a later age, be experienced by those initially trained in the hard but often materialistic schools of science and technology? Is it possible for a nation to develop such a thing as the technocratic mind in a ruling oligarchy? If this is possible what safeguards ought we to introduce to prevent the ascendancy of such a cast of thought? How in short can we bring it about that those who wield such forces as those opened up by nuclear physics come to realise that they must sooner or later, and of their own volition, bind themselves by some new 20th-century version of the Hippocratic oath to use their knowledge solely in the service of mankind? And what have those concerned with education to contribute to such a consummation? At the end of Britain's first Industrial Revolution thoughtful people everywhere were echoing a phrase attributed to Robert Lowe (though he actually said something rather different[1]): 'We must educate our masters.' May not 'We must humanise our masters' become an equally insistent 'slogan' as this new Industrial Revolution unfolds?

At the end of the war the 'Percy' Committee, one of the strongest and most knowledgeable Departmental Committees which has ever examined the country's provision for Higher Technological education, came to the conclusions: first, that the position of Great Britain as a leading industrial nation was being endangered by a failure to secure the fullest possible application of science to industry; and second, that this failure was partly due to deficiencies in education.

About the same date it was estimated that a sum of at least £50 million would have to be spent on the buildings and equipment of new Colleges of Technology over the next 15 years.

In the ten years which followed the Percy report, successive Governments in co-operation with the Local Education Authorities and through greatly increased financial aid to the Universities did in fact take such substantial strides along various lines of action which the Committee recommended that in many respects the outlook by 1955 was beginning to look considerably more heartening.

By the session 1954–55 for example the number of full-time students (64,000) attending Institutions of Further Education was more than three times, the number of part-time day students (402,000) more than four times, and the number of evening students (1,575,000) half as large again as those in the last pre-war year—the figures for which would be the ones examined by the Percy Committee. £22 million worth of new Technical College buildings had been completed by Local Education Authorities with a further £16 million worth 'on the stocks'. An annual programme

[1] His actual words were: 'We must at least persuade our future masters to learn their letters.'

of £6–£8 million was receiving approval. Simultaneously the 23 British Universities had spent on new science buildings £13½ million plus another £7 million for equipment out of their Parliamentary subventions.

Nevertheless to the outside observer this advance, however substantial, still tended to present the appearance of having resulted from a somewhat piecemeal and haphazard response to a largely unco-ordinated demand rather than from a clear-cut and intelligible plan deriving inspiration and leadership from the top to achieve definite national targets within given periods.

Indeed the thoughts passing through the mind of, for example, a friendly Canadian observer of the English scene as it stood in 1955 might well have taken some such form as the following: 'During the first Industrial Revolution England was clearly in the lead and of recent years she has played an outstanding part in many forms of basic research in electronics and nuclear physics.

Faced by this new Industrial Revolution, however, which is bearing down upon all industrial nations, others certainly seem to have been quicker than the mother country to appreciate that the nation which will stride ahead will be that which best solves the problem of stepping up the supply of Scientists, Technologists, Technicians and Craftsmen.

Russia claims to be training every year 35,000 professional scientists and 65,000 engineers. That represents 508 per million of her population. In addition she claims to be turning out 141,700 high-grade technicians annually. Moreover she is talking of stepping up these figures as rapidly as possible. Our neighbours in the United States are producing 23,600 graduates in pure science and 22,600 graduates in engineering and other technologies annually. This represents 280 per million of her population and, with her eyes on the Russian effort, she is aiming at doubling her output of engineers by 1964. Western Germany is producing 86 graduates in technology per million; Sweden 82; France 70; and Italy 30.

In the free air of Canada one may well entertain private reservations about some at least of the Russian claims. To Western and American eyes technologists are educated persons in the broadest sense (which involves a substantial capacity for original and independent thought). Is the Russian school system one under which independent and original thought is fostered? Certainly the popular impression in the West is that behind the Iron Curtain independent and original thought has too often hitherto been regarded as dangerous thought. Opinion in the United States appears to vary from the extreme of those who accept and are deeply alarmed by every Russian claim and the cynics who aver that one Sputnik does not necessarily mean a Technologists' summer; and that nations which have carried the arts of propaganda to such an extreme point of efficiency as Russia may be greatly tempted to use statistics as a bad motorist uses his headlights—to dazzle rather than illuminate the road ahead.

All the same all the evidence available does seem to show that the quality of the Russian output is high and the proportion of the national budget set aside for education (£8,420 million) and science (£2,500 million) is a sixth of the total. Similarly one may well entertain some reservations about the quality of some at least of the American product, especially if one studies the "Report on Universities and Industry" produced by a special team of representatives of British Universities, Colleges of Technology, Industries and H.M.I.s who visited the U.S.A. in 1951 under the auspices of the Anglo-American Productivity Council.

By contrast when one comes to examine the British output of professional scientists and technologists last year (1954–55) one finds it was 240 per million—less than half the Russian claim and substantially below that of the U.S.A. These figures hardly seem reassuring when one recalls that 40% of Great Britain's working population is in manufacturing industry and particularly if one knows the clamant needs of the Commonwealth for British trained scientists and technologists.'

Turning from this general background picture in an attempt to isolate and pinpoint those features which seemed to have acted as a brake on our progress, hitherto the same Canadian observer would probably have continued his soliloquy along the following lines:

'England's conservative cast of thought has for too long given her a predilection for aiming at a high standard of education for a limited number of "flyers". The old "night school" tradition dies hard as does the conception that higher technological education can recognise and be confined within the strait-jacket of highly artificial local government boundaries.

She has developed excellent "Polytechnics" each offering a regular cafeteria of courses at all levels and this has certainly made the entry to Technical education more flexible than is the case in most other countries. Nevertheless the job of these Institutions too often appears to have been conceived as that of bringing educational first aid to those whose abilities might have carried them forward to the University, had they not fallen by the wayside too early in their school careers and been forced to climb the ladder to professional status by the hard way. England therefore has still to realise the need for Institutions of Science and Technology which can offer courses leading to qualifications equal in standing to and comprising a comparable amount of study to those leading to University honours and postgraduate degree courses. This would present the additional advantage that such courses could avoid the rigid conformity with the Faculty requirements for external degrees of London University. To expand the 23 Universities themselves, or add sufficient new Universities to undertake a job of such dimensions, would clearly be out of the question owing to the time factors involved. Clearly, too, the mother country will have to break down the embargo which one Local Education Authority can still place on the attendance of a student from its area at higher technological courses in an adjacent area.

Again she ought to break once for all with the old "night school" outlook. It is asking too much of human endeavour to expect that Technologists and Scientists of the stamp and breadth of outlook looked for today can get all they require by years of evening study after a day's work and still preserve that resilience which they will need. There must too be a real swing in emphasis from part-time courses to periods of full-time education interspersed with full-time work in industry; from evening classes to part-time day release classes of a purposeful character.

Finally British Industry and the Trade Unions must somehow be convinced as a whole, before the sands run out, that "Trade follows Training" and that to encourage selected employees to follow advanced courses will be in the best interests of the nation as well as of immediate gain to the employee and his particular works. The Government needs to make the aims and structure of Technological education readily intelligible in every Board Room and Trades Union office.'

The purpose of directing this strong spotlight on the position as it existed in 1955 is that it is from that year that the future historian may be able to date the awakening of England to the perils of underestimating Science and Technology.

As the Venetian Ambassador to the Court of St. James reported to his masters so long ago as the year 1500, no people are more ready than the English, once they are aroused, to seek that road along which they may best serve their interests. Correspondingly we are, of course, incredibly inarticulate in explaining what we are about. As Kipling put it:

> 'For undemocratic reasons and for motives not of State,
> They arrive at their conclusions—largely inarticulate.
> Being void of self expression they confide their views to none;
> But sometimes in a smoking-room, one learns why things were done.'

It is probable that at any time during the year 1955 an eavesdropper in the smoking room at the Athenaeum or the Oxford and Cambridge Club might well have heard all the points put into the mouth of our imaginary Canadian.

Parliament and the English public had to wait a little longer. For it was not till February 1956 that the Government's new policy was launched in a memorable White Paper (Cmd. 9703). This announced a five year plan (1956-61) to cost £70 million for Technological building and £15 million for equipment; set a production target of 15,000 advanced course students a year by 1966; outlined the Government's intention to name a number of leading Regional Colleges of Technology as 'Colleges of Advanced Technology' which would involve their shedding all but advanced course students and thus husbanding for courses of 'honours' degree standard the scarce teaching power of their highly qualified staffs and the availability of their expensive equipment; enunciated clear definitions of the terms Technologist, Technician and Craftsman; expressed it as the Government's aim to double the number attending day release classes; and enjoined generosity in the provision of county major awards and other forms of training grants upon the Local Education Authorities, and equivalent generosity in facilitating the release of apprentices and other staff for educational courses upon both sides of Industry.

In the University field a massive expansion of Imperial College of Science and Technology was promised to raise its student numbers from 1,650 to 3,000 at a cost of £15 million; and an indication was given that the Treasury would look with a more than ordinarily sympathetic eye upon developments in the Universities' facilities for scientific and technological education then under discussion between the University Grants Committee and the several Universities for the quinquennium 1957–62.

This ambitious programme should, if it can be achieved, raise our annual output of technologists and applied scientists who, usually after further study, obtain membership of one of the professional Institutes (M.I.M.E., M.I.E.E., etc.) to about 23,200 or 215 per million by the mid 1960's and probably 330 per million if one adds the 'pure' scientists, many of whom enter industry. It has been estimated, for example, that by 1966 Britain will need 11,000 chemical engineers of graduate status. This 330 per million, it will be noted, will still be short of the present Russian claim although we shall probably have kept pace both qualitatively and quantitatively with the United States and other industrial nations. At the University level (where student choices have always been remarkably sensitive to prospective demand) the numbers in the scientific and technological faculties are expected to rise to 55,000 or say an output of 15,700 a year by 1966 and most of these should obtain professional status whereas on past experience about half of the annual 15,000 from the Colleges of Technology should also do so. The figure indeed becomes considerably more heartening when one recalls that the pool of professional scientists and technologists already at work in a country which has been producing them for many decades must be considerably greater in proportion to population than that available in countries which entered the field more recently. The existence of this pool is too often forgotten by those who fix their eyes too rigidly upon current annual production. White papers and blue prints, however stimulating, are not, of course, the same thing as solid achievement. Nevertheless the drive which has been put into implementing the Government's proposals—by the Ministry, by the Universities, by the Local Education Authorities, by the National Council for Technological Awards under Lord Hives' chairmanship* and by both sides of Industry—has deserved success even if it eventually falls short in one or more respects of ensuring it. Indeed in examining the record of what has been achieved in the first three years one is reminded of the old proverb 'Well begun is half done'. Already, too, there is evidence that the English system of technical education is developing a more clear-cut and orderly outline which can be understood by the employer and trade unionist alike, an understanding which has gone far to improve the climate of opinion about the imperative need for rapid development.

Eight colleges of advanced technology (colloquially referred to throughout the English educational world as C.A.T.S.) have been designated and relieved of non-advanced work. Three are in London: Battersea, Chelsea, and the Northampton College in Clerkenwell. The others are at Cardiff, Birmingham, Bradford, Loughborough and Salford. New buildings and extensions at these eight colleges have absorbed ten out of the 70 million. Two others, the Bristol College of Technology and Rutherford College, Newcastle, are likely to be designated as soon as certain conditions have been fulfilled. This will improve the national coverage geographically.

These eight colleges are developing buoyantly and it is encouraging to find how many school leavers who would in former years have thought in terms of 'the University or nothing' are enrolling in their courses, particularly those for the Diploma in Technology. This Diploma was instituted by Lord Hive's National Council for Technological Awards and the conditions for the approval of courses were first settled only in 1956. The award will be of University Honours degree standard and may well confer upon its possessors the same kind of cachet as that which Lord Trenchard's police college conferred upon those members of the force who were lucky enough to 'get in on the ground floor'.

The Council has gone to work with such a will that by the end of 1958 seventy-seven courses with nearly 1,800 students were in operation in the C.A.T.S. and the Regional Colleges of Technology. Sixty-two of these courses are what is known in the 'jargon' of the world of education as 'sandwich' courses, that is to say courses in which a student already employed full time in industry attends the advanced technological course full-time for six months of the year and continues this six-monthly alternation between industry and full-time education over all the years of the course. A variant is that where six-monthly jobs with industrial firms are arranged by the College to alternate with a student's full-time education.

This sandwich system, though of great antiquity, has 'caught on' remarkably since the White Paper of February, 1956, the 100 such courses with 2,300 students of that date having swelled to 321 courses with between 9,000 and 10,000 students in the 1959–60 session. It will probably however have to rise to over 600 courses with 15,000 to 20,000 students to provide the 6,000 advanced students a year from this type of course looked for by 1966.

The successful launch of the Diploma in Technology has already prompted the Hives Council to look forward to the creation of a further award equivalent in the field of Technological Education to those post-graduate degrees (e.g. D.Sc.) to which a proportion of honours students at the Universities aspire. This new award will be named Membership of the College of Technology (M.C.T.) and will be obtainable only after an interval of responsible experience in Industry.

Lest it should be thought however that no dark anxieties disturb the calculations of those responsible for such substantial progress, it is necessary to face frankly the probability that (except at Loughborough) there are unlikely to be enough hostel places before the end of the first decade to enable every student for the 'Dip. Tech.' to 'live in' for at least one year of a full-time course or one session of a 'sandwich' course; that the problem of attracting teaching staff of the very highest quality to fill vacancies for senior appointments has proved a stubborn one; and that the

Colleges still (1959) have a long way to go in developing research, post-graduate work and liberal studies.

These bottlenecks fuse together and intertwine. A College can exist without sufficient hostel accommodation, it can carry its students forward along formal technological studies with a comparatively limited number of staff of first-rate quality; it can even undertake a limited amount of research for Industry. It cannot burgeon and flourish under such conditions. To achieve parity with the University Departments of Science and Technology it must be able to offer to those students who join it with strong side interests, for example in economics or politics, music, drama, painting or photography, the college union debates, college societies, special lectures and so on which the Universities can offer. Similarly, if it is to attract to Senior lectureships its proper proportion of those first-class brains which can unlock the minds of it students by tutorials and command rather than invite applications for help with research from local industries, it must be able to offer such staff salary inducements, standards of accommodation and amenities comparable to what they would enjoy in a University atmosphere.

It should be added that many of the other difficulties which beset advanced students before 1955 have been mitigated or removed. For example 'free trade' between the Local Education Authorities in admissions of students to Colleges in other areas has been ensured by a financial 'pooling' device and the number of State Scholarships and major county awards to those proceeding to Universities has probably increased from about 4,500 in 1954–55 to over 8,000 in 1958–59 with a comparable increase in awards to those entering senior courses at technical colleges from 3,395 to 7,656.

As against the £70 million building programme adumbrated in the White Paper £22 million had been completed, a further £71½ million was on the stocks and £37 million had been approved by the end of 1958, the Government having announced a further programme of £54 million to be completed in the years 1961–64.

Before concluding this brief glimpse at what has been described as the revolution now taking place in this country's provision for scientific and technological education at the higher levels, it should be recorded that the Universities—which stand outside the Public Educational System and so outside the scope of this book—are meeting similar expansive pressures.

The rising tide between 1955 and 1958 can be illustrated in tabular form as follows:

ENGLAND, WALES AND SCOTLAND—NUMBER OF STUDENTS

	Universities		Institutes of Technology					Total
	Pure Science	Technology	Dip. Tech.	Degree	Higher National Diploma	College Diploma	Others	
1955–56	17,500	11,200	—	2971	2279	1616		35,566
1957–58	21,707	13,850	1391	3576	3927	3691		48,141
Autumn Term 1958	23,000	15,000	1786	—	—	—		—

Nearly 40% of the total student body at the Universities is now concentrated within Faculties of Pure and Applied Science and if this proportion is maintained as the University population grows to 127,000 in the mid sixties the number of science and technological students may well become 55,000 (probably 28,000 technology and 27,000 science) an increase of about 86% on the number in 1955.

As has been indicated above, a technologist is one who has the qualifications and experience required for membership of a professional institution. He must possess a firm all-purpose mind and be an initiator expected to push forward the boundaries of knowledge in his particular field. As such he must be preserved from the unessential for the essential, as any science master will appreciate who in the absence of adequate assistance in his school laboratory has to fritter away his time in setting up apparatus.

Are we, therefore, making comparable progress in the training of technicians—the installation and maintenance engineers, plant and test operators, draughtsmen, assistant designers, technical assistants and junior ranks of management on the shop floor?

In the U.S.A. three to five technicians are considered necessary to support every professional technologist. Some authorities in this country would put the figure even higher and a good deal of disquiet has been expressed from time to time as to whether we may not be building a pyramid which will not support the weight of its top courses.

Supposing, for the moment, that we do succeed in swelling the roll of those winning through to membership of the professional institutes to say 23,000 a year by the mid sixties we shall need for their support at least 100,000 technicians, men who, to reduce the matter to its simplest terms, have been trained to understand what they are doing, why they are doing it and how it can be better done.

What are our chances of obtaining such a number annually?

Our present output is difficult to assess. A limited number of highly trained technicians is produced annually from those who do not proceed to obtain the necessary endorsement for membership of a professional institution after completing a Degree course, a course leading to the Diploma in Technology or one of those conferring a Higher National Diploma or Certificate. It is probable, however, that not more than 5,000 out of the output of advanced courses in 1958 (11,000) fell into this category.

A further supply comes from those taking the full technological examinations at the technician level of the City and Guilds and other examination unions. The City and Guilds numbers increased by 84% to nearly 7,000 between 1951 and 1957 and appear to be growing by about 7% annually which should bring them to 10,000 by 1963. An even more rapid increase is apparent in the case of some of the other examining unions.

The substantial question therefore remains: what further proportion of the 43,500 and 342,000 students who were in 1957–58 attending respectively full-time and part-time courses at senior and advanced level in preparation for work related to specific industrial occupations will emerge as technicians? At the time of writing (1959) the *cognoscenti* seem to be about equally divided between those who see no difficulties in achieving such a goal as 100,000 a year and those who can see nothing else. It is for example alleged that the optimists tend too readily to think in terms of the nationalised industries and the 'blue chip' industrial giants forgetting the 40,000 industrial units in this country which employ less than 100 workers apiece. These small firms, it is argued, may take a paternal interest in their young workers but it is asking a great deal of them that they should release them in large numbers to take full-time or sandwich courses. For the cost to a firm of training a worker up to Diploma in Technology level may be as much as £1,400. Unless, therefore, the Government is prepared to step in and organise a group apprenticeship and block release scheme, or to put up substantial capital to provide apprenticeship training centres like that established at Cachan in France or in Solingen—the Sheffield of Germany—the small firm will prefer to purchase the technicians it needs from those trained by the large industrial organisations. Others quite rightly point the warning that the production of technicians and technologists goes right back to the Primary School—some would say the Infant School. Only about one third of the laboratories in grammar schools, it is alleged, can be said to be generously equipped, another third are only adequate and a third below standard. In far too many cases too the 'Mr. Chips' of the grammar school common rooms must perforce staff these laboratories in the absence of young recruits. Up to 1956 it can be shown that only 19% of the 11,500 graduate mathematicians in the country were not professional teachers. From that year a progressively increasing proportion of those graduating has been drawn away to Industry, which is becoming more and more statistic and computer conscious. Even the seasonal revisions of our railway time-tables, to make the best use of line capacity, rolling stock and train crews are now the work of computers. They seem indeed to be attaining much the same hold on the imagination of some of the captains of modern industry as the Delphic Oracle and the Shrine of Jupiter Ammon held for the captains of the ancient world—sometimes it is unkindly suggested supplying answers nearly as inscrutable!

Furthermore, it is asserted, nobody can forecast the rate at which the demand for technicians may expand. Automation alone may affect five million of the 24 million employed in our manufacturing industries during the coming decade. Its operating techniques may call for the employment of half a million qualified technologists and technicians. On a working life of thirty-six years this would postulate an annual recruitment of 14,000. The optimists on the other hand pin their faith—and it is a broadly based one—on their knowledge of current trends in the secondary and independent schools and the evidence of an increasing readiness in Industry to anticipate its long-term needs for trained personnel. The outside world can, as yet, only measure the response of the schools by such indications as the 77%, 137% and 120% increase in passes in mathematics, physics and chemistry as between the General Certificate of Education results at ordinary level in 1951 and 1958; the 94%, 78% and 53% increases in the same subjects at advanced level; the rise from about 75,000 to well over 100,000 in the number of pupils attending Secondary Technical Schools or in the Technical streams in Bilateral, Multilateral and Comprehensive Schools.

The administrative staffs and inspectorates, central and local, know, however, how fundamental a reorganisation of secondary education has been taking place since 1955 in many areas to provide five, six and seven-year courses; the extent to which heads of secondary schools are becoming conscious of the impact of science and technology upon the ambitions and requirements of their pupils; what a high proportion of the secondary school roll is now staying on at school after 15; how the proportion of pupils in science sixth forms is increasing annually; of what immense service to industry an efficient secondary modern school can become if its technical side is closely geared to and co-ordinated with the pre-senior National Certificate courses in the local technical college.

Industry too, after what appeared to many to be a long uphill struggle to wean it from its attachment to doing things in the way that past experience had shown to be adequate rather than to experiment with new ideas which might prove to be better, is now turning enthusiastically—especially on its engineering side—to the sandwich course principle. Perhaps, comparing the product of such courses with those produced by the system of student apprenticeship with part-time day release for the technical studies which was almost universal in 1955, managements are finding that the slower assimilation of theoretical knowledge between longer intervals of working experience on the shop floor is giving them recruits with that grasp of the fundamentals over the broadest possible range which in the past they have almost unanimously demanded but not always obtained.

As one of the earlier manifestations of this increasing interest, the Industrial Fund raised by a number of the larger Industrial Groups enabled the independent and direct grant schools to improve their facilities for science teaching to the tune of £3 million. A similar interest in the cultivation of fields too long parched by the disappearance of the private benefactor and the pious founder has led to the creation of a number of Industrial Scholarship schemes. The best of these, such as the Trevelyan Scholarships, are designed to ensure greater breadth of study among candidates for University places.

In the summer of 1958 a tripartite Industrial Training Council was established representing the British Employers Confederation, the Trades Union Council and the Boards of the National Industries. The first move of this Council has been towards the appointment of training officers to stimulate the formation of training and apprenticeship centres, group apprenticeship and block release schemes.

Most important of all, the British Employers Confederation at a special meeting on 21st April, 1959, committed themselves to two principles. First that their members should take on for skilled trades in each of the three years 1961–63 20% more boys than they had recruited in 1958; second that employers organisations should undertake the responsibility for giving a central lead in training matters generally for their industry, and for working out training schemes for all their young entrants, both boys and girls, so that these training schemes can be in operation by the beginning of 1961.

If this initiative is followed up with vigour, and more particularly if it leads to apprenticeship coming to be regarded as a problem of training rather than of employment, it may go far to solve one of the most disquieting shadows which for some years has been haunting those concerned with education and industry. This has been the fear that the injection of vigorous young men and women which the 'bulge' age groups might confer on our economy might be lost through a failure to step up the increase in our intake and training of apprentices from the present annual figure of about 95,000.* How necessary this will be will be appreciated by anyone who studies the figures. For the average number of boys and girls in England, Wales and Scotland reaching the age of 15 over the three years 1961–63 will be 869,000 as compared with the 712,000 of 1958.

Lord Eustace Percy, who as Minister of Education in the 1920's always seemed, in his thinking about the country's economic future, to be 30 years in advance of all but a few of the most far-sighted Industrial leaders and Principals of Technological Institutions, used to stress first the need for a radical and large-scale reorganisation of our education for the engineering industry, second for a new concept of our education for salesmanship.

In this respect history is now repeating itself, and in the next few years we shall probably see a considerable expansion of our provision for commercial education, education for management and facilities for our representatives to improve their knowledge of the countries and languages of our potential customers.

Some observers from abroad are said to be quite amused by the hypercritical attitude that the British adopt towards their efforts in the field of technical education. Yet the suggestion is still often heard that the managements of British industries are less alert to apply new scientific discoveries or machinery than their American counterparts. This is a fertile field for debate rather than one in which it is possible to reach any overall conclusion. The critic can cite numerous past failures to develop some industrial process in which pioneer work was done by British scientists. Good examples would be the subterranean gasification of otherwise unproductive coal seams;* our loss of the watchmaking industry in which we once held a high place; our production of cars to Italian body design. His opponent will produce an equally formidable array of examples of highly ingenious industrial applications of up-to-the-minute knowledge. He might cite, for example, the cutting of the thickest plate-glass to any shape by ultrasonic waves; the vista opened up in India and the Middle

TECHNOLOGICAL AND FURTHER EDUCATION

East by the stabilisation, freezing and reconstitution of Pasteurised milk, giving it a life of 18 months, again by ultrasonic means; the scores of ingenious industrial applications of radioactive isotopes.

Probably it would be true to say that our longer industrial history and experience of unemployment between the wars makes us more cautious than our friends across the Atlantic in circumstances where a transformation of technique may create human problems. We are notably less ready to proclaim epoch-making discoveries in the field of medicine or surgery until we have proof of their efficacy over a number of years.

In our placement procedure the work of the Central Scientific and Technical Register of the Ministry of Labour reinforcing that of the University Appointments Boards is probably as effective as, though less spectacular than, the work of the American Alumni Associations and 'Campus recruitment' carried out by the high-pressure job salesmanship methods of industrial recruiting sergeants.

In general, the rewards now offered to those possessing good scientific and technological qualifications, and to designers for industry, a profession which for long failed to secure proper recognition, are very much higher than they were between the wars.

Almost everything which has been said in this chapter hitherto has been concerned with our provision for education for livelihood, personal and national. What provision does our system of Further Education make to assist the individual in the business of living the fullest possible life within the limitations set by citizenship in a modern industrial democracy?

Between the wars Further Education was often spoken of as 'Education for Leisure'. This phrase does not seem so satisfying as it used to, now that we live in a world divided by conflicting ideologies. In such a world survival of a distinctive way of life may ultimately depend upon the building up of a sufficiently high proportion of individuals in every community who are capable of recognising Propaganda as the 20th-century successor to oratory in the rôle of 'harlot of the arts'. The majority of adult members of the community in Britain today enjoy considerably more leisure than was the case 40 years ago. Their basic need seems to be a sufficiently wide range of opportunities to follow any individual cultural urge, however humble, to a point where this culture, in the mass, will present an adequate bulwark against the undermining of their remaining liberties with their heritage of beauty and independent thought. Anyone who has lived abroad for some time and returns to this country will recognise that as a people we are probably as kindly, as genuinely solicitous for the welfare of the under-privileged and as sound in our resistance to being pushed around against our will as any race on earth. Such a remark as 'Of course mere amenity must never be allowed to interfere with efficient farming' will at once be subjected to a humorous, profoundly good-tempered, but devastating riposte in *Country Life*. We are still too, thank God, a very long way from the kind of technocratic disregard for the individual which one encounters in Hitler's *Table Talk*. Moreover those who in science fiction phantasy foresee the Government of Britain being taken over by a Cabinet of electronic brains can still be comforted by the assurance that there are probably not yet as many valves and transistors in the world as there are neurons in a single human brain.

Yet the depth of feeling in the six words 'Where now are these satanic mills' of Blake's 'Jerusalem' have a special significance for the social historian who has read widely and deeply about the first Industrial Revolution and its effects. He must be a brave man if he can view with complacency the immensely more powerful forces which may be unleashed in the new Industrial Revolution upon which we are now entering. Even the man in the street cannot observe without growing anxiety the kind of propaganda which is already directed in the name of 'progress' against the citizen who, for example, questions the rights of those who break the sound barrier above his head or drive at 100 miles per hour along the roads for which he has paid.

Already occasionally one may encounter the thesis that the scientist's conscience is as other men's; and that as the keeping of the common conscience lies in the Government's hands he need suffer no qualms in carrying out Government orders. Those who put forward such arguments may be genuinely shocked when asked if they would condone the frightful medical experiments perpetrated on the inmates of Hitler's concentration camps.

There is a school of thought which holds that good citizenship is a plant which will grow of its own accord if it is given the appropriate soil in which to spread its roots. Good housing estates provided with community centres backed by social security and genuine secondary education for all should, or so the adherents of this school of thought argue, make good citizens of all of us.

In the opposite camp are those who believe, with Plato, that guardianship of the common weal can only with safety be entrusted to men and women possessing an intellectual maturity founded upon an education co-extensive with life. Such an education must, they argue, embrace in its field of studies religion, art, science, philosophy and the institutions of government and society.

Modern educational opinion experiences some difficulty in subscribing wholeheartedly to either thesis. It knows what an uphill struggle housing managers in the new towns have experienced in starting community activities and building up a community consciousness against the competing claims of television, the garden plot and tinkering with the family car or motor cycle. It knows, too, that Plato lived in an intellectually élite society based on slavery and not a democracy whose citizens must achieve citizenship despite the limitations imposed by the width of the wave-band of academic aptitude.

It sees the spread of automation progressively reducing the number of jobs calling for strength and rhythm and of purely repetitive jobs requiring speed and dexterity. It must therefore endeavour to keep as many young people as possible at school after 15 in the hope of setting them on the road to becoming craftsmen and technicians. Nevertheless it must recognise that those who leave school at 15 must somehow be persuaded to join an evening institute in the hope that through its activities, however humble at first, they may in time be led to experience some cultural urge.

'What proportion of the population,' it may well be asked at this point, 'ever responds to an individual cultural urge unrelated to its work?' Unfortunately it is extremely difficult to provide a satisfactory answer owing to the coy reticence with which the available statistics classify as '21 or over' every evening student who has attained a latchkey whether he is a future Cabinet Minister, an intellectually mature grandfather, or merely an aspiring band leader.

What can be demonstrated is that in those areas which like London have made it a point of honour to endeavour to satisfy every cultural demand the proportion of each age group up to 60 which will be found enrolled, season after season, in evening classes is by no means negligible. For if one plots on a graph the 265,000 students it will be found that they form a rough triangle from 15 to 60.

Such a graph will also indicate that full-time attendance and part-time day attendance at technological classes appear to diminish nearly to vanishing point by the age of 30. This supports a belief held by those who have studied the matter that ambition as a motive force tends to give way after the years in which men and women are concerned with carving out a career, establishing a home and raising a family. In their view it is often replaced after 30 by studies undertaken with a broader cultural aim. These are selected to fill some self-realised vacuum of the spirit on the humanistic or speculative side of education, to expand an interest in drama, music or art, or to improve the style of the student's home or dress.

When one comes to ask oneself how far there is evidence of an increase in the demand for classes specifically designed to satisfy this 'second flowering' at the higher intellectual planes, however, it must be admitted that the answer is disappointing. There has been a threefold increase since the last pre-war year in the number of students in Musical Appreciation classes. A few thousand more students are studying History. On the other hand Philosophy, Political Science, and the History and Appreciation of Art have remained stationary. They are apparently not subject to a rising tide comparable to that witnessed in the technological and scientific subjects. Students of English have declined from 271,000 to 251,000.

This, however, is only one side of the picture, for it must be remembered that the number of 'Arts' students at Universities has over the same period increased from 22,500 to 41,121. There has, too, been a welcome expansion of almost every type of University Extension and Tutorial class provided by the Universities, the Workers Educational Association and the Joint Committees for Adult Education in Devon and Cornwall.

It would, too, be a profound mistake to assess the importance of the 159,611 students enrolled in Adult Education courses in 1958 (as compared with 57,000 in 1937–38) merely in terms of the relatively insignificant proportion which they form of the total adult population. The leaven of culture which those who have pursued such courses succeed in diffusing among the mass of the population can justly be compared to the influence of Cluny in the monastic world of the early Middle Ages.

If the problem of the past 50 years has been to prepare the nation for 'secondary education for all', that of the next 50 is going to be to expand the cultural education of the mind and spirit as a life-long process. Adult education must 'fan out' from those who have hitherto been prepared to seek it to those who have hitherto been indifferent or uninterested. To achieve this we shall have to bring about something of the same revolution in our thinking about what is a proper form of adult education for the untouched masses as we have achieved in our thinking about methods of unlocking the mind of the 'modern school' child.

---

*p. 90: Sir Harold Roxbee Cox became Chairman on the retirement of Lord Hives at the end of 1959.
*p. 98: The number of school leavers becoming apprentices or learners was 110,564 in 1958 and rose to 119,332 in 1959. Both figures are roughly 21% of the number of school leavers entering employment.
*p. 98: Subterranean gasification was first referred to as a possibility by Sir William Siemens in 1868 and was the subject of experiments by Sir William Ramsey in Durham in 1912–13.

IV

THE WELFARE SERVICES OF ENGLISH EDUCATION AND SCHOOLS FOR THE HANDICAPPED

THE PREOCCUPATION OF ENGLISH EDUCATION WITH THE WHOLE LIFE OF THE CHILD. HOW THIS AROSE. SOME ACHIEVEMENTS OF THE MATERNITY AND CHILD WELFARE AND SCHOOL MEDICAL SERVICES. PRESENT DIFFICULTIES. THE SHORTAGE OF HEALTH VISITORS. THE VALUE OF THE VOLUNTARY WORKER. THE SCHOOL MEALS SERVICE. THE HANDICAPPED CHILD. HOPE FOR THE FUTURE. THE VARIOUS TYPES OF HANDICAP. NEED TO WORK FOR A HIGHER 'QUALITY' OF LIFE IN A FITTER AND BETTER EDUCATED POPULATION.

ONE of the features of English education which nationals of other countries usually experience some difficulty in understanding is how the public service of education cheerfully accepts responsibility for and carries so many welfare services, and the extent to which it concerns itself with the whole life of the child and the interaction between home and school.

To the English social worker or teacher it has come to seem almost axiomatic that the school child should be periodically medically examined by a School Medical Officer; that he should receive medical or dental treatment at a clinic maintained by the Local Education Authority; that after illness he should be transferred from an ordinary primary or secondary school to a school of recovery; that he should be referred to a child guidance clinic and from that to a school for the maladjusted maintained by the Authority; that he should be provided, through the school organisation, with mid-morning milk and a midday dinner; that he should be fitted out by the same organisation with boots and clothing if his parents cannot afford to send him to school warm and dry; that he should be advised in school how to join an evening play centre or enrol in a youth club; that he should be interviewed in school about choice of employment; and finally that he should have his bus or train fare paid if he lives more than a prescribed distance from school.

Yet an English educational administrator or teacher may encounter complete mystification when speaking to a conference of educationists drawn from more logical countries where a Ministry of Public Instruction probably concerns itself strictly with schooling as such while a Ministry of Social Administration spreads its mantle over the deprived and delinquent, old people, the tuberculous and alcoholic, resettlement and labour problems.

It is open to question whether the English educational system would eventually have absorbed to itself so many interesting social offshoots had the product of the monasteries and chantries at their dissolution been applied to the development of that respectable network of Ancient Grammar Schools which was already in existence by the 16th century. It has, for example, been calculated that in 1546 there was one such school for every 8,000 of the population (then roughly 4,000,000). A comparatively small infusion of the wealth of the monastic lands and possessions at that time, when a salary of £20 a year probably commanded a purchasing power of £1,500 today, would almost certainly have rendered us educationally the leading country in the world. The subsequent development of our school system might in that event, however, have assumed a very different complexion. Quite possibly it would have exalted that erudition with a classical stamp which became such a marked characteristic of the country landowners of the late 18th and early 19th centuries. Instead it had to be built up hurriedly from the bottom as a species of 'Good Samaritan' first aid to illiterate masses.

In the event the rapid expansion of the child population completely outran the supply of schools. This expansion followed upon the hastily improvised public health measures called into being to prevent the spread of such diseases as cholera among the urban conglomerations brought into existence by the first Industrial Revolution.

The Ancient Grammar Schools, it is true, continued to exist

and here and there to expand. Nevertheless even where they were located within reach of the new concentrations of population, their resources and endowments were wholly inadequate to cope with the demand for school places produced by the improving fertility and survival rates.

In writing of the currents of popular opinion which have contributed to the ebb and flow of educational history broad generalisations are best avoided, or at least hedged round by exceptions. But, with this cautionary proviso, public education for the mass of the nation's children does seem to have been widely thought of initially in terms of first aid for children who might otherwise grow up without access to the Bible; later as a charitable duty to combat poverty, squalor and vagrancy in the young, which might lead to vice and unrest as they grew older; and later again as a means to produce disciplined (and therefore amenable) factory hands, railway workers who had a sufficient capacity in the 'three R's' to avoid piling up the trains, and junior clerical labour for commerce.

At the other extreme there were idealists of the stamp of Robert Owen in plenty. The historians of education have done full justice to them. It is probably a mistake, however, to overrate their influence on their immediate contemporaries.

At each stage enlightened but frustrated reformers working in the actual schools did, however, see clearly the impossibility and the utter wastefulness of their task. So long as a high proportion of those for whom a place in school could be found at most for a few years were prevented from staying the course by poverty, hunger, *or* disease or the ignorance, squalor and idleness of their parents any real progress towards a system of public education as it is understood today must proceed at a snail's pace.

Thus it came about that the development of public education in our great cities presents a constantly recurring pattern of initial voluntary effort by pioneers of vision being taken up and imitated elsewhere until it reaches the Statute Book. It has usually done so first as a 'power' and ultimately as a duty laid upon Local Educational Authorities by Parliament. For example, the pioneer work of a few teachers who organised penny dinners for school children in the last two decades of the 19th century led to permission being accorded by Parliament in 1906, as a result of a Private Member's Bill, to assisting the provision of such dinners to the extent of ½$d.$ rate. From this small beginning we have arrived after two world wars at the acceptance by every shade of political opinion of the principle that school meals should no longer be confined to necessitous children but available as of right, and as part of the social security programme, for all children whose parents desire it and are prepared to pay the very moderate charge representing the cost of food (less administration).

Other examples are the special schools for the handicapped, the first of which was opened by voluntary effort nearly 200 years ago; medical inspection and treatment of the school population; Mrs. Humphry Ward's evening play centres; the provision of boots and clothing; and the measures taken since the 1939 war, largely as an outcome of experience gained by the voluntary Child Guidance Clinics of pre-war days and during the war itself through the Government Evacuation Scheme, for the early detection and treatment of psychological maladjustment which so often leads to ultimate delinquency.

In the 40 years between the inception, on a national scale, of the School Medical Service in 1908 and the commencement of the National Health Service in 1948 it is not too much to say that, under the vigorous direction of Sir George Newman and his successors, it became one of the two foundation stones of the national health. The country had to wait 10 years until 1918 before the second was laid. In that year the efforts of the pioneers in the welfare of mothers and young children (mainly concentrated initially in the northern industrial towns) was recognised in the first Maternity and Child Welfare provisions in a Public Health Act.

Upon these twin foundation stones was erected that fine superstructure of public health services which stood up so well to the strains imposed by the Second World War. In combination they have created a national health conscience which was almost non-existent at the commencement of the century. This has been instrumental in the cutting down of maternal mortality from 4,000 deaths, representing 6 per thousand births in 1900, to

328 in 1958, representing ·43 per thousand births. It has been the driving force behind the reduction of the death-rate of children in their first years of life from 154 per thousand in 1900 to 22·5 per thousand in 1958, a figure nearly as good as those in such well-housed countries as the Netherlands (17·2), Sweden (15·8) and Norway (20·5).

With its support the percentage of the child population immunised against diphtheria, which was as low as 2% so lately as 1939, had been raised to 54% in children under five by 1958, thus cutting the number of cases annually from 65,000 and nearly 3,000 deaths in 1938 to 80 and only 8 deaths in 1958. Such figures even looked at as a cold 'business proposition' mean that in return for an expenditure of about £50,000 a year on initial propaganda a sum of two to three million must have been saved every year in hospital costs besides the services of at least 2,000 nurses.

Although the Maternity and Child Welfare services fall outside the scope of a chapter on the welfare services of public education the effect of such achievements as these on survival rates and so ultimately on school population will be evident to anyone who studies the figures on page 169.

It would be extremely interesting, if it were possible, to illustrate the scope of the changes which have been witnessed by the school doctors since the inception of the School Medical Service by showing what a School Medical Officer and School Dental Officer examining 1,000 children would have found in the early years of the service and what he would find today. Changes over the years in the methods of recording the findings of school medical inspections unfortunately make this an almost impossible task for a layman. For example, there has clearly been a tendency, while school dentists have been in short supply, to concentrate attention mainly on children referred as appearing to need urgent treatment to relieve pain. This puts up the proportion of those found to be in need of treatment as against the total examined.

Again, definite malnutrition has virtually disappeared and the tables now record the 'general condition' of children under the three heads of 'good', 'fair' and 'poor'. Similarly, part of the

THE WELFARE SERVICES

reduction in the number of children receiving operative treatment for enlarged tonsils and adenoids may be due to an increasing belief that a minor degree of enlargement may be a peculiarity of an individual child's growth which may right itself. Moreover such operations are commonly discontinued when cases of poliomyelitis are occurring.

The following table should accordingly be examined with reserve as representing no more than an attempt to obtain a general picture from the available statistics.

Findings at routine medical examinations of 1,000 children in 1908 compared with estimated findings in 1958:

	1908	1958
1. Dirty in varying degrees, that is with nits in hair or body lice present	140	40
2. Dental treatment necessary	800	686
3. Nose and throat defects (e.g. enlarged tonsils and adenoids)	150–180	30 requiring treatment 67 requiring observation
4. Malnutrition	130	17 general condition "poor"
5. Diseases of the heart and circulation	30	2 requiring treatment
6. Diseases of the lungs	10–30	7·9 requiring treatment 22·2 requiring observation
7. Ringworm	10–20	2·08
8. Rickets	40	nil
9. Defective footwear	100	negligible
10. Inadequate clothing	50	negligible

If comparison is made, on the basis of the Registrar-General's vital statistics, of the number of deaths which occurred as a result of the main killing diseases of childhood, namely measles, diphtheria, whooping cough and scarlet fever, one will find that on the basis of 6 million children under fifteen 15,432 deaths were attributed to these diseases annually up to 1910 as compared with a mere 102 in 1957.

It would be an exaggeration to say that the improvement in the statistics of child health is solely due to the public health and school medical services. One half of the world is so little aware of the conditions in which the other half lives that educated people will open their eyes in pained surprise if they are reminded that for example in the London borough of Shoreditch, so late as 1938, 68% of the children had no facilities for bathing at home and 15% were sharing the available water supply with three or more other families; that in Hull and Bootle 40% of houses were without baths at the outbreak of war; that in Stepney it was 90% in the same year, and so on. No country in the world has so good a housing record as Great Britain since the end of the First World War, for we provided in England and Wales alone 4,267,549 new homes between January 1919 and March 1945 and have raised this number by a further 3,500,000 since the end of Hitler's war. We must therefore have found new homes for well over half the population in 40 years, and, although we lost 222,000 houses by bombing during the war, clearly the health statistics reflect the fact that as a people we are becoming better housed. We are still, however, not appreciably ahead of the Netherlands or Scandinavia. Other contributory factors have, no doubt, been the distribution of welfare foods to expectant mothers and to children under five, pasteurised school milk and school dinners, improvements in drainage and refuse disposal, hospitalisation, sulphonamides and antibiotics and general health education.

The actual movement of public opinion which brought the School Medical Service into existence as a statutory service in 1907 is something of a gift to those uncomfortable individualists who attempt to trace past medical or social reforms to the working of a guilty conscience in a people with markedly Puritan antecedents. A few years before, the appalling total of 21,000 Boer women and children had died of epidemics in the camps into which they had been concentrated. This shocking page in our history is now better remembered on the Continent than in this country. Hitler made diabolical use of it in the film *Oom Paul*, produced by his propagandists to inflame Nazi youth. In fact, the sufferings of these women and children deeply stirred the national conscience and made the Englishmen of the day—still only partially awake to social needs—notice the conditions under which far too many women and children were living on his own doorstep.

There were, too, other and more practical arguments in favour of instituting medical supervision of the child population (which had existed partially in London since 1890 and in Bradford since 1893). The country had been shocked by the number of recruits it had been found necessary to reject on medical grounds. It was also rather ingenuously believed that medical inspection would be an inexpensive means of obtaining an anthropometrical survey of the population and of persuading parents to take their children to a family doctor or hospital for treatment. When the Local Education Authorities were squarely confronted by the mass of defects indicated in the table above, and also by the discovery that parents did not, in fact, seem at all disposed to besiege the hospitals and doctors' surgeries on receiving a slip of paper informing them that Tommy had ringworm, necessity compelled them to take action. First in back-street Minor Ailment Clinics and dental surgeries often opened initially by voluntary effort, later by a steadily expanding network of treatment centres for visual and aural defects, by X-ray treatment of ringworm, by rheumatism clinics, sunlight clinics and arrangements with local hospitals they gradually built up a medical service which was probably without parallel over most of the rest of the globe.

In 1948 every parent in the country became entitled to select a family doctor under the National Health Service scheme and secure treatment for themselves and their children free of cost. By that year the School Medical Service was employing the equivalent of 831 full-time School Medical Officers, 880 school dentists, 944 dental attendants, 2,366 school nurses, 212 district nurses and 195 nursing assistants and conducting approximately 3,000 treatment centres and clinics. In addition, arrangements for meeting the cost of operative treatment for enlarged tonsils and adenoids, serious diseases of the ear and treatment of ringworm by X-ray existed in practically every area of the country.

Although there can be no question of the ultimate advantages which the National Health Service will confer on the population as a whole it is too early yet for a layman to estimate whether it will spell advance or retrogression in the more limited sphere of securing prompt and effective medical treatment of the school population.

Some School Medical Officers seem to view the new prospect with considerable misgiving. They welcome, it is true, the readiness with which the majority of parents today attend school medical inspections. On the other hand they cannot forget the *laissez-faire* attitude adopted by the less educated and more casual mothers of earlier generations and the pressure which had to be brought to bear upon them to bring their children for treatment. They have the best possible reasons for knowing that such mothers still exist. Moreover, when responsibility for treatment rested on their own shoulders they had the means to ensure that it was in fact carried out. When the Local Education Authority paid the local hospital for an operation or examination it could insist on receiving those full reports which are quite essential to any adequate follow-up of treatment and recovery, especially where, for example, the report indicated a need to admit the child to an open-air school or secure remedial exercises in school.

The Regional Hospital Boards and not the Local Education Authority now appoint the specialists and arrange hospital appointments for children. If, as is alleged, they are sometimes proving casual about the loss of school time and secretive (on the grounds of breach of medical confidence) about keeping the Local Education Authority informed of what is happening, it is understandable that some School Medical Officers should feel that apart from the school clinics which they still maintain they have lost control of that section of the school treatment service which was based on hospitals. The final word on any expansion of this branch of the service must appear to them to have been taken out of their hands and to have been placed in those of bodies not controlled by popular election. Yet the public, who elect the Local Authority which employs them as School Medical Officers, will, they feel, hold them responsible if treatment is not provided or for dreary hours spent by children waiting their turn at hospitals. Finally they wonder whether the child with some apparently minor defect, such as post-nasal catarrh, which may lead to much trouble later, will, in fact, receive the same meticulous care in future as he did in the school clinic in the past.

The Ministry of Education has every reason to be proud of the School Medical Service and it is to be hoped that action to cure such teething troubles is proceeding behind the scenes, as it probably is.

The School Dental Service was nearly brought to an untimely end by the determination (as it appeared to the outside observer) of an impetuous Minister of Health to start a National Dental Service when only 8,000 dentists were available as against the 18,000 required. It is now recovering, but even at its darkest hour the Ministry of Education took a very firm line with those who suggested that the Local Education Authorities should refer children found by the school dentists to be requiring treatment to the surgeries of private dental practitioners. The purpose of the School Dental Service, they pointed out, was to provide a comprehensive service of regular inspection and treatment of school children—an essential feature of any scheme for the conservation of the teeth. The most effective way of ensuring that the maximum number of children obtained regular treatment was the provision of a dental service closely associated with the educational system. Moreover, the influence of the teachers, undoubtedly the greatest single factor influencing the attitude of school children towards dentistry, was likely to be more effectively exercised when the dental service was organised in this way. All these arguments would—or so it would appear to the lay observer —apply with equal force to that section of the school medical treatment service which is carried out through the Hospitals.

Another, and potentially more serious because less easily remediable, threat to the school health services is the chronic shortage of health visitors. Outside the Metropolitan area the school nurse health visitor can become the king-pin of the service. Locally she can become the eyes and ears of the School Medical Officer, she is the chief executive in the school treatment service,[1] and she is usually the welcome confidante and friend of the child's

---

[1] In London, School Treatment Organizers, who are trained social workers, carry most of the executive work of treatment and much of the liaison with hospitals.

home. This fact was recognised in the post-war flood of roseate social legislation by a proposal (embodied in Section 24 of the National Health Service Act) to extend her orbit and functions to the health of the family as a whole. Up to that date they had been largely confined to Maternity and Child Welfare, the School Medical Service, and tuberculosis visiting.

Whether those who framed the Act made any calculation of the number of health visitors required to implement this section, or to examine the possibility of attracting into the service a sufficient proportion of the product of the girls' grammar schools after meeting not only the wastage of health visitors due to marriage and so on, but also the competing claims of the teaching profession, the Universities, industry, commerce, agriculture, and the Government and Local Government services, is not ascertainable. The best material available for an estimate was provided by a nation-wide research carried out in 1950 by the Nuffield Provincial Hospital Trust, who thought that 560 families per health visitor would be an appropriate case load. Since there were 13,043,000 families in England and Wales at the 1951 census this would postulate a force of 23,000 health visitors.

A report produced by the Women Public Health Officers Association in 1952 suggested that 11,000 would be necessary to cover adequately the needs of the Maternity and Child Welfare and School Nursing services. This target was confirmed by the Departmental Committee on Health Visitors which reported in 1958.

As against these requirements the statistics published in the annual reports of the Ministry of Health show that the total is barely half the 11,000 required and that the training courses are barely replacing the annual wastage.

Those who plan social advance in a modern democracy would do well to take stock, at every stage, of the ability of the nation's schools to produce staff with sufficiently high initial educational qualifications to man any new service they propose, especially where, as in this instance, they are in practice limited to one sex. A Welfare State, like a biological species, continually tends to move from the unspecialised and undifferentiated to the specialised and differentiated.

THE WELFARE SERVICES

The Welfare Services, which are or should now be available to every family in England and Wales, are indeed so varied and all-embracing that it is doubtful whether any individual who has not taken at least a two-year post-graduate course in the Social Science Department of a University, followed by some years' experience as a professional social worker, can have more than a working acquaintance with a limited proportion of the field they cover. How to bring precisely the right agencies to the assistance of a family in trouble while avoiding overlapping and waste of effort has, therefore, become a major administrative problem in the offices of most local authorities. It is a problem which is being tackled in a variety of ways: for example, through co-ordinating committees of local authority officers, representing the medical, health visitor, education, housing and children's departments, through citizens' advice bureaux and through co-operation between voluntary societies.

An extremely interesting, though at present unique, organisation of this type is the care committee organisation which has grown up over the past 50 years in the London area. This organisation is expressly designed to make sure that nothing in any child's physical or mental make-up or home surroundings shall hinder him or her from receiving full benefit from the services provided under the Education Acts. At every school a committee of voluntary workers, working in close partnership and consultation with the teachers, collectively make it their business to know the home of every child and see that every appropriate form of assistance is called in aid where home difficulties are handicapping a child in getting the most out of his school days. These voluntary workers, who now number 2,400, are recruited, trained and advised by a small body of permanent and salaried organising staff, all of whom are professional social workers. Each voluntary worker receives his or her appointment direct from the Education Committee and undertakes to give some fixed proportion of his spare time to the work. Many of them are retired head or assistant teachers or retired professional social workers.

The London clergy and their wives, professional parish and settlement workers, form another large section; but probably the largest group of all is that composed of educated wives and mothers, who can find a few hours each week for the kind of voluntary service which, as all who have experienced it know, invariably brings its own reward. Although certain specific duties are laid down for care committees in their orders of reference, of which the assessment of families for school meals free or at reduced cost, the operation of the boots and clothing scheme and the follow-up of medical inspection are the most important, the scope and variety of unostentatious help of other kinds rendered to London families every year by these individuals, who are accepted as family friends, is beyond computation.

The sum of the services given by the 2,400, of whom over 600 are men, adds up to the equivalent of 400 full-time workers.

In view of the scope and complexity of the forms of assistance now available in the Welfare State and the shortage of professional salaried staff to administer them, it is somewhat surprising that this system, which has attracted much interest abroad and has been copied as far afield as Japan, should not have been more widely followed as yet in the rest of the country.

The *School Meals Service* is now so much an integral part of the life of all schools and so well known that little need be said about it. It now ensures a well-cooked and nutritionally well-balanced daily dinner for more than half the school population. The price charged represents the full cost of the food, but overheads are excluded. Children whose parents are adjudged unable to pay the full cost can receive dinners at reduced cost or free. Thus it reaches all those children whose nutritional needs were not always adequately met in the past. Indeed in its early days 'I'm not used to having a Sunday dinner every day' was a remark quite commonly heard in school.

Its educational value has been two-fold. In the first place it has trained children to accept as palatable and as a matter of habit meals containing in concentrated form all the various food values which a growing child needs. This, in combination with the work of the School Domestic Science Departments, undoubtedly accounts for the notable changes in dietary patterns in the modern home observed by those who conduct consumer surveys. In the second place it has afforded a valuable additional opportunity to give unobtrusive social training. If table manners are not learnt during school days they may never be learnt at all by a proportion of the population. It is to be hoped that as the whole school population becomes rehoused in up-to-date schools with their own dining-rooms and kitchens the sad little crocodiles which are now too often encountered on their way to an outlying meals centre will disappear. Irish stew on a sloping desk is poor substitute for a well-laid-out dining-room with formica-topped tables and well-arranged flowers from the school garden.

It is fatally easy for anyone who has never been brought into close association with the nation's *schools for handicapped children* to imagine that they must form a depressing no man's land peopled by unhappy children who feel themselves to be in some way different from their fellows in other schools, physically or socially outcasts, or pushed on to the side-lines where they are at best objects of compassion. Nothing in reality could be further from the truth. Compassion there is, of course, but it is a practical compassion sublimated into a determination, which has become second nature to the very fine and devoted body of teachers attracted to this service, that never by word or action, by loss of patience or by letting any child suspect the difficulty of their task, shall they allow a child to lose heart, still less lose hope.

Hope indeed is the word which springs most readily to the mind of those who have been the longest in touch with the problem. For the present situation is one that is full of hopefulness. Indeed, the present generation of administrators and doctors can already feel a reasonable confidence.

In the next 50 years we will probably make as much progress in immunisation and inoculation in operative, obstetrical, pharmaceutical and radiological techniques, in psychiatry and electronic devices as we have in the past 50. If we do so there should, by the end of the century, be practically no totally blind or totally deaf children to educate, virtually no partially deaf, partially sighted or epileptic children who cannot attend ordinary schools, very few cripples, or children with tuberculosis of bone or joints and a greatly reduced number of constitutionally delicate children. On the other hand, it is probable that the number of educationally subnormal children will be much the same as that today, and there will still remain a substantial number of children who will have to undergo training for speech defects and psychological maladjustment.

Favus, trachoma, ophthalmia neonatorum, rickets—to mention only a few of the conditions with which school doctors of an earlier day had to contend—have gone. Tuberculosis and osteomyelitis are on their way out. Even poliomyelitis (which still kills less children every year than cancer) is now yielding to immunisation.

On the other hand, if one passes from the contemplation of what eventually may be to the hard facts of today it is a sobering reflection that the 60,000 children in upwards of 1,000 schools for the handicapped[1] still represent the total population of sizeable towns such as Bedford, Burton-upon-Trent, Chester, Folkestone, Guildford, Harrogate or Lancaster, or the total school population of such counties as Buckingham, Leicester, Wilts and Monmouth or such large towns as Kingston-upon-Hull, Nottingham or Stoke-on-Trent.

That is not to say that if they were all assembled together in the schools of one of these towns or counties the casual visitor, unaware that they had all been ascertained to be handicapped, would necessarily notice anything strikingly different between them and the ordinary school population they had replaced. In fact, if he encountered a group of them in the public baths and they did not happen to be a group of spastics or children exhibiting definite malformation of the limbs due to one of the variety of other crippling conditions, he might think they were a group from any ordinary school. Even totally blind children when their training has been on the right lines will walk about on stilts, swim or trot freely round a gymnasium avoiding obstacles

---

[1] One still encounters here and there an impression that except in London and the large towns the chance that a Local Education Authority will secure an appropriate education for a handicapped child in a special school is so poor that School Medical Officers refrain from 'ascertaining' anything but the most urgent categories. Those who give currency to such opinions should revise them by reference to the facts. The truth is that the Local Education Authorities in co-operation with each other and through the voluntary societies have increased the number of special schools by nearly 500 (from 528 to 1,014) since the war. The most serious shortage which remains is schools for the educationally subnormal.

by some uncanny sixth sense. The partially sighted can usually only be distinguished by the thickness of the glasses they wear. The deaf are no longer 'dumb' as they were 30 years ago. The maladjusted and the epileptic have no physical peculiarities and a layman who encounters for example a physical training or dancing period in a school for the educationally subnormal, from the name of which this label will now have been removed, will, as likely as not, be astonished to be told that they are not perfectly normal youngsters.

One further general point is worth recording before examining the variety of types of handicaps for which special school provision is made. This is that the amount of thought which is now given by the Youth Employment Service of most Local Education Authorities to finding interesting work which a handicapped school leaver can do despite his or her defect is beyond praise. The days when the virtuosity of blind or crippled craftsmen was used as a kind of shop window device to attract the contributions of the compassionate have happily departed. On the experience of recent years 98% of the 7,000 children in London's special schools for the handicapped can look forward to obtaining work which will render them self-supporting, and, what is far more important, self-confident citizens. It is especially heartening to find, as one sometimes will, a handicapped worker doing a job which could not be done at all by a worker with no handicap whose training has followed the normal lines. For example, it is possible to discover a blind shorthand typist sitting in the X-ray room of a hospital where she can take down *in the dark* notes dictated by the radiologist as he examines patients at the fluorescent screens. Similarly deaf children will work in a room full of mechanical computors the noise of which can be very trying to those with full hearing.

Fortunately only about one child in 4,000–5,000 nowadays has no sight or sight which is or is likely to become so defective that he requires education by methods not involving the use of sight. The figure is, however, liable to variation. This is not, happily, because anything foreseeable or preventable in the existing state of medical knowledge is occurring to raise the number. It is because from time to time new medical or pharmaceutical techniques are developed which may, until they are perfected after experience, result in saving the lives of children who formerly would have died, but failing in the process to prevent blindness or deafness. Examples occurred in the early days of the application of the new sulphonamide and antibiotic drugs in cases of meningitis and more recently in the case of premature babies kept alive in the earlier type of oxygen tent.

Before 1948 tuberculous meningitis was invariably fatal. Since the introduction of streptomycin mortality has been reduced by 70%, but the antibiotic itself may produce deafness in some of the survivors.

The actual educational methods and the wide range of special Braille books and maps and other teaching apparatus required in the training of these sightless children clearly postulate residential education throughout their school career and the earliest possible start. This start is usually made at the age of 2 or 3 in one of the Sunshine Homes for Blind Babies—where even the colour schemes and pictures are so designed that the joy they give to the sighted visitor may be communicated to the children. Passing to a residential school for the blind about 5, the normal blind child will remain in full-time education till 16, although in nearly all cases further full- or part-time education will carry them on to 19, 20 or 21. Since all parents of special school children are naturally preoccupied about them, and none more so than the parents of the blind, a residential school which can be easily visited by the parents is a *sine qua non*. It has therefore been the object of the Ministry of Education since the war to bring about as good a distribution of such schools as possible in relation to the 'scatter map' of the children's homes.

Anyone who has visited or seen films taken at schools for the blind or examined the records of those who have passed through the two fine secondary grammar schools for blind children at Chorley Wood and Worcester will probably feel that all is now well with the imaginative care and training afforded to that class of child which is most in need of all that education can give to it.

In addition to those children who have to be taught through Braille and other methods appropriate to the sightless, there is a somewhat larger number of *partially sighted*. These cannot follow an ordinary curriculum without detriment to their sight or their educational development, but can still be educated by special methods involving the use of sight. The incidence per thousand of such children seems to vary considerably from area to area. It used to be put at about 1 child in 2,000, but in some parts of the country seems to be as low as 1 in 3,300 (·03%) and in others as high as 1 in 1,350 (·08%).

The young partially sighted child of primary school age needs very special care, not only because special pains must be taken not to let him do anything which may damage his eyes in later years but because he will probably be awkward. And, as any psychologist knows, nothing is sadder than the clumsy child who may become a butt for other small children or a cause of impatience to an unknowing adult and who seeks to protect himself by buffoonery or exhibitionism. Posture, too, is of importance for many types of partial sight, as is also the avoidance of fine handwork and certain types of physical exercises. Some teachers of partially sighted children, though not all, believe that a compensatory retentiveness of memory is evoked by the handicap of partial sightedness.

It follows that the earlier the parent of a partially sighted child can be brought to realise the value of securing special education for him in a school staffed by understanding experts the better will it be for his emotional development and ultimate attainment. The transformation which can be brought about in a year or two in a partially sighted child who has been attending an ordinary school and is transferred to a special school has to be witnessed to be believed.

Much research has been carried out both in regard to the prevention of partial blindness and into educational devices for its amelioration. As an example of the first the discovery made in Australia during the Second World War, that if a woman contracts German measles—up to that time regarded as the most insignificant of infectious diseases—during the first three months of pregnancy there is a possibility that the child when born will be partially blind or partially deaf, has opened up a promising field for investigation. As an example of the second may be mentioned the evolution of portable and adjustable table lenses which will enable most partially sighted children to read—for spells of 20 minutes—print of all normal school types. Equipped with such lenses they can often, after training in a special school at the primary stage, pass on at 11 to the ordinary secondary school.

About one child in 2,000 is so *deaf* as to have no hearing or hearing so defective as to require education by those methods evolved for children who would in previous ages have remained dumb because they would have been unable to learn to speak through hearing those about them doing so. In the days when a deaf child was shut off from all means of communication with the outside world except sign language and finger spelling there were those who regarded deafness as almost a greater affliction than blindness. Today the situation is much happier owing to the progress which has been made in the teaching of lip reading and the development of electronic aids which enable the 75% of deaf children who have some residual hearing at some tone or frequency to hear the teacher's voice and so learn themselves to speak with a natural intonation. In many schools for the deaf classrooms are now wired so that the children are in radio telephonic contact with the teacher and can move about freely or dance to music.

Here again, as in the case of the blind or partially sighted child, the education of the parent is of paramount importance. Anyone who witnessed the remarkable film *Mandy* will recall the boredom and frustration of the deaf child denied its birthright of admission to a school for the deaf at the earliest possible age and the handicap imposed on the teacher by any delay in admission. Indeed it is now known that deafness and partial deafness can be detected in a child as young as nine months by a health visitor who has received a short course of training. A very encouraging movement is afoot to concentrate on training any residual hearing in these deaf babies and toddlers from 9 months to 2 years by admitting their parents to residential hostels where they can learn the technique. Work on electronic devices and transistors has enabled a satisfactory baby's hearing aid to be devised by the use of which a deaf toddler can enter at two on the nursery school stage of his education much more fully alive to the world around him and more readily educable than in the past. One of the saddest features of the education of the 25% who are totally deaf hitherto has been the tendency for their background knowledge and attainment to fall progressively behind that of normal children until by fourteen they may be two or three years retarded, a gap which cannot be wholly closed by their retention at school till 16.

This development of hearing aids has without doubt revolutionised the teaching of the *partially deaf* in recent years and enabled many of them to pass into the ordinary secondary schools after education in a special class for partially hearing children at the primary stage. Some still require, however, to attend a day or residential school for the partially deaf, and it is a happy feature of the new situation brought about by hearing aids that probably for the first time all the partially deaf who need special education can be found an appropriate place in school.

What the elimination of trachoma and ophthalmia neonatorum has achieved over the years in the reduction in the number of blind children to be educated and the development of hearing aids has done for the deaf seems to be paralleled in the case of the *physically handicapped*, including the class of children previously known as 'pre-tubercular' or 'delicate'.

The varieties of physical handicap for which special school provision has to be made are of course a matter about which no layman is qualified to write. All that he can do is to record impressions. These can be summed up by saying that in the past 25 years many of the worst crippling conditions which used to scourge the child population seem to have vanished. No doubt they have been reduced to a fraction of their former incidence by orthopaedic surgery in the earliest years of many children's lives.

He will still encounter a number of serious heart cases due to rheumatism or other causes, although modern therapy, better housing, drainage and sanitation have probably reduced the overall total by 25% to 33% as compared with 10 years ago. Moreover, at many schools he may be told of children who were, seemingly miraculously, able to return to an ordinary school perfectly fit after undergoing, for example, an operation which enabled the valves of their heart to close properly. Rheumatic fever is, however, one of those 'lurking' diseases of which we may witness a recrudescence.

He will pass on to examine progress in bringing tuberculosis under control in the child population and will find that on the basis of 6,000,000 children aged 5-14 no less than 4,752 died in 1907. By the outbreak of the Second World War he will find that the number had fallen statistically, still on an assumed 6,000,000 children, to 960 (the actual figure in 1938 was 973). He will turn to the figure for 1957 and find it was 30.[1]

Statistical inference from records of deaths is hardly perhaps for many people a heart-warming process. What is much more encouraging is the current evidence of the reduction in the risk of a child today coming into contact with a sufficient concentration of tubercle bacilli to prevent his natural resistance throwing them off without trace. It is therefore most heartening to find that whereas in 1949, 30% of London children aged 13 showed evidence by the 'tuberculin skin test' of having met and reacted to tuberculous infection, the figure for this same age group tested in 1954 had fallen to 15%. Pasteurised milk supplies are manifestly yielding a dividend, but the incidence of new active tuberculosis tends to appreciate rapidly in the 15-25 age groups, an argument which might well be addressed to those employers who still fail to understand the importance of works canteens.[2]

In the years since the war a great deal of attention has been directed, too, to that class of physically handicapped children usually referred to as spastics. Spasticity or Cerebral Palsy, most often the result of some brain injury at birth, varies widely in the degree of its severity. Many spastics, for example those who exhibit no more than some minor degree of impairment in the movement of a limb, can and probably should be allowed to take their place with other children in the normal school population. Too often the most serious cases used before the war to seem almost hopeless, although those pioneers who know most about

[1] 8.7% of all children who died under the age of 14 in London in 1900 died of tuberculosis. By 1950 it had fallen to 4%.
[2] In the age group 15-44 years the proportion of all deaths which is attributable to tuberculosis has remained around 30% throughout the half century.

them, for example at Queen Mary's Hospital at Carshalton, argued unceasingly that they would often prove to be of the highest intelligence if only they could be educated in the control of their rigid muscles. Here again, as with the deaf and partially sighted, the education of the parents is of vital importance, and interesting work is being done at Newcastle—and no doubt elsewhere—to begin the work of restoration in infancy and to train parents how to follow out the appropriate regime and remedial exercises.

Thus physical handicaps which to earlier generations seemed almost as though they had been ordained by nature are gradually yielding to orthopaedic surgery, new operative techniques, cleaner milk supplies, remedial exercises, better housing, drainage and sanitation. The over-all picture can be illustrated by saying that many years ago accommodation seemed to be needed in special schools for the physically handicapped for from 5–8 per 1,000 of the school population, of whom 1·5 per 1,000 would be children for whom education must be arranged in Hospital. Today the proportion has come down on the basis of a nation-wide survey undertaken by School Medical Officers to 2·15 per 1,000, indicating a need after allowing for the same proportion in Hospital of only 1·65 per 1,000 for whom special school places are required.

This, be it noted, is the real reply to those tiresome individuals who still ask whether we are not today saving thousands of child lives only to produce a generation of weaklings. For the term 'physically handicapped' embraces all those children who in the past had to be admitted to schools for the delicate and schools of recovery.

The incidence of *diabetes* in the school population is fortunately not high. Probably there are 1,500 diabetics in the total school roll of six and a half million. This would give a proportion of one in 4,333. Many of them can be educated without difficulty in ordinary schools. A few have the malady in such an acute or unstable form that they must, for their own safety, become permanent hospital patients. Probably not more than 150 need to be in residential special schools or hostels from which they can—with the establishment of an ordered regime of diet and insulin injection—go daily to ordinary primary or secondary schools.

E

The management of such a school or hostel imposes great responsibilities on the staff, who must be highly qualified both on the nursing and the child care and dietary side. Every ounce of food has to be weighed before it is eaten and an intelligent but mischievous youngster can soon, for example, get the idea of giving himself an extra dose of insulin if he has been taking unauthorised liberties with the sweet ration! Those who have devoted themselves to the service of the diabetic child will usually call attention to the noticeable proportion who are in the higher intelligence groups. Whenever a special school or hostel is found to be the right course for a diabetic child he or she should be admitted to it with the minimum delay. It is necessary to persuade the parents to appreciate that where every child is on a level in disability with all his fellows he soon learns to make light of it. Even children of five or six will be found in such schools administering insulin injections to themselves and thinking nothing of it.

Palliative medical and pharmaceutical treatment of the *epileptic child* has made such strides in recent years that the less seriously afflicted are today much more readily accepted in ordinary schools than was the case a few years ago. This is especially true when the child comes from a reasonably good home and has been free from fits for one or two years.

The incidence of epilepsy in the school population has been the subject of a great deal of research and on the basis of a survey of 1,700,000 children in the year 1946 and 1947 was until recently put at 1 in 3,300. A more detailed survey carried out by the Ministry's Medical Officers in 1950–51 on the basis of 355,000 children raised the figure to about 1 in 800. The need for special educational treatment only seemed, however, to be indicated in about one case in six (1 in 4,700 of the school population). On this basis the number of special school places existing or in process of being provided in the country as a whole is probably now sufficient and may even allow for a few unfilled beds.

The suggestion is sometimes heard that many of the best-known names in world history would be found to have been borne by epileptics. The names usually canvassed are those of Pharaoh Akhnaten, Julius Caesar, St. Paul, Galileo, Napoleon,

Dostoevsky and Lenin. It has even been suggested that the cerebral irritation associated with epilepsy in their case may, as it were, have stepped up the voltage of their brains. The present expert view appears to be that so far from epilepsy being associated with genius about 10% would be found to be below and about 15% fewer above the intelligence norms established for the ordinary population. Modern opinion seems, too, to have discounted the old theory of an 'epileptic temperament'. Undoubtedly many epileptics display unusual behaviour symptoms, but this may be due to maladjustment arising out of their home environment or a feeling that they are society's 'odd man out'. To the layman epilepsy must always seem, as it seemed to the ancient world, one of the most appalling visitations to which any human being can be subjected. Anyone who has read their letters home will find himself torn between admiration for their cheerful acceptance of their lot and compassion for their burden.

The most he can hope is that epileptic children enjoy compensations which enable them to live in the present to a greater extent than might be supposed. But there can surely be no one who has encountered epilepsy at first hand who does not wish God-speed to the encephalograph and the armoury of new drugs now available for its relief.

Educationally subnormal children form a comparatively large and, until recent years, much misunderstood section of the school population.

Intelligence testing by methods designed solely to measure academic aptitude normally achieves some such spread of the population as the following:

Intelligence Quotient		
130+	... ...	1 per cent
110–129	... ...	22 ,,
90–109	... ...	52 ,,
70–89	... ...	22 ,,
below 69	... ...	3 ,,

If this spread were set out like the wave-band dial or scale on a radio set the educationally subnormal group would be found in that section falling below 75 or 80. A small proportion in the lowest section of the scale would be ineducable and for these the term 'mentally defective' is now reserved. This term in less enlightened times used to be applied to the whole category and no doubt accounted for the regrettable attitude too often adopted by thoughtless people towards such children. It is a curious fact that boys outnumber girls in the schools for educationally subnormal by two to one. Perhaps girls are more easily dealt with in the ordinary schools, but there are some grounds for believing that they tend to occupy the middle sections of the wave-band of intelligence and score less freely than boys in the higher and lower groupings. Here it is necessary to emphasize that, although the techniques of mental testing have made remarkable strides in the past 30 years, those who know most about the subject would probably be the last to claim that the tests most commonly employed do more than indicate certain aptitudes which are likely to be useful in tackling the ordinary school subjects. Moreover, the score obtained on a given day may vary as much as 10 points as a result of health, social or emotional factors. Tests designed to assess such factors as a child's emotional stability, persistence, temperament or ability to get on well with his fellows will no doubt in time become more reliable as experience accumulates. The contribution which a good home can make to the development of such qualities is of great importance.

Again, it should be noted that nearly every member of the population possesses some idiosyncrasy of physical or mental development. If we find ourselves in a psychologically closed environment, one where we feel we may not be welcome or are excluded from the life around us, these idiosyncrasies may affect our behaviour. Anyone who has read E. M. Forster's *Passage to India* or recalls the behaviour of some of the mothers who were evacuated into other women's homes at the outbreak of war will appreciate this phenomenon. It was particularly noticeable in some of the British families living in the German scene but not of it during the post-war phase of occupation. Clearly it accounts for much of the 'peculiar' conduct attributed to those suffering from mental disability.

If nature suddenly decided that no baby born in future should be of an intelligence quotient less than 130, most of us would find as we grew older that we were regarded as morons!

It is therefore of the first importance to provide the right environment for any child who feels that he is 'odd man out', and may start to behave accordingly. For the educationally subnormal child this must be an environment where he will meet with sympathetic understanding; receive individual treatment in a school class smaller than that in the ordinary school; have his strong points studied; and be led by the development of those qualities in which he is nearest to normality to a point where he can stand on his own feet in the world. Both common humanity and economic expediency point to such special treatment as his birthright; for if he is not equipped at school for the responsibilities of adult life he may well become, sooner or later, a much heavier charge on the community as an inmate of a mental colony, a Borstal institution, or a prison.

If he is so equipped there is no reason why he should not become literate enough for the ordinary affairs of life, agreeable to live with, a steady and well-liked workmate. In a hard world he may find employment readily and be quite content to work as a member of a team or on repetitive processes which would be purgatory to a man of high intelligence.

Too many people perhaps make the mistake of being unduly sorry for the child born educationally subnormal but not sufficiently sorry for his parents to appreciate how much help they may need in adjusting themselves to accept his disability. It is no kindness to such parents to suggest that he is probably only temporarily retarded and will presently shoot forward; or that some wonder drug may soon be discovered which will ensure him a place in a grammar school overnight. It is much wiser to help them to realise that educationally subnormal children are born to people in all intellectual strata. They must have it explained to them that no cure or palliative is yet known to medical science (except in the case of those babies whom a simple test in the first two months of life discloses to be suffering from phenylketonuria: these can be saved from the mental deterioration, otherwise inevitable, by a special diet). Nevertheless as parents they can help their child's emotional development enormously by providing him with a loving home and being guided by the advice of the School Medical Officer and the Head of the nearest appropriate school.

Unfortunately the supply of schools for the educationally subnormal still lags far behind the need except in the larger urban areas.

At the end of the war of 1939–45 the Ministry of Education recognised a further type of handicap: *maladjustment*. Experience which had been accumulated in the hostels for children who proved difficult to billet with ordinary householders during the wartime evacuation had confirmed the findings of the pre-war Child Guidance movement and led to a realization that substantial numbers of children—some of them among the most intelligent—fall by the wayside quite unnecessarily. The psychologists in the Services who had encountered these children at later ages had been shocked at the human wastage they represented.

The maladjusted child can be described as one who shows evidence of marked emotional instability or psychological disturbance and requires special educational treatment in order to effect his personal, social or educational readjustment. It is easy for anyone who has never had an opportunity to study the case-papers of such children to wonder whether the educational world is not pursuing a will-o'-the-wisp in believing it is possible to distinguish the cases of genuine and severe maladjustment from those of children who are merely suffering from an overdose of indulgent or heartless parents; and to effect a cure. Even if he were given the case-papers of three or four hundred such children he might still, after reading them, form the conclusions, first, that maladjustment can arise from so many different factors that it must be well-nigh impossible to diagnose the principal causes in any given case; second, that an enormous number of children must be maladjusted in some degree. Fortunately neither conclusion would be valid, for the normal child seems to be a tough organism and will usually stand a great deal of hardship and unwise treatment; and the causes, though legion, do tend to fall into a number of patterns which the experienced psychologist can piece together.

This is a field which the layman must enter with caution, but he would probably find if he were to study a large number of reports upon individual cases that the commonest ingredients seem to be the following (it should be stressed, however, that the last thing a Child Guidance Clinic would do would be to attempt to fit a child into a particular category before reaching an independent diagnosis):

Factors related to the child's home surroundings
  (*a*) Loss (e.g. through the death of parents or break-up of the home) of the normal relationships of a good home.
  (*b*) Uncertainty as to the future continuance of such normal relationships (e.g. illness or drunkenness in the home, transfer of parental affections).
  (*c*) Frequent change of home background.
  (*d*) Frustration (e.g. lack of outlet for ambition, interests and energies).
  (*e*) Failure of the parent or parent-substitute to give proper home training, example, or balanced nutrition.
  (*f*) The positive influence of bad homes (e.g. tuition in petty thieving or more serious anti-social activity, active dislike or cruelty).
  (*g*) Psycho-neurosis arising from some circumstance (possibly accidental) related to the home.

Factors related to the constitutional make-up of the child himself
  (*a*) Inability to acquire knowledge, or particular types of knowledge, with the same facility as his fellows (e.g. through mental retardation, whether genuine or brought on by ill-health or social factors). This may lead to an attempt to compensate by abnormal behaviour or inability to adapt himself to life in an organised society.
  (*b*) Physical inferiority (such as clumsiness arising from some disorder of sensation, locomotion, or sight; metabolic or glandular disorders affecting his psychological attitude; deformities or inferiorities which again are liable to lead to an attempt to compensate by peculiarities of behaviour).
  (*c*) Inability to keep in step with the group, or to feel or make judgments like an average member of society, leading to a feeling of inferiority.
  (*d*) Functional or organic distortion of mental processes with

secondary alterations in his attitude to other individuals and to society in general.

(e) Moral defects such as inability to acquire any outlook beyond an egocentric one. These are often combined with distorted emotional and pleasure-seeking impulses.

To anyone unacquainted with their work it may seem fantastic to suggest that the Child Guidance team of psychiatrist, psychologist and psychiatric social worker can hope to restore a broken home, convert a drunken stepfather or reform a Fagin. Yet these are the kind of successes which are often achieved. It may be doubtful whether it can hope to do more than delay the ultimate break-down of a definite psychotic. It can discover and put right many of those cases where some physical cause is transmitting continual messages of discontent to a child's brain. Above all, it can establish the presence of and try to eliminate such factors as a feeling, conscious or sub-conscious, in the child that he does not matter to anyone; that he is inferior mentally or physically to his fellows; that he has been the victim of injustice; that he must get even with or outdo some other child; that he has no outlet for his energy or ambition; that other members of the family are preferred to him; that he must escape from his surroundings; that he is the 'butt' of others; or that his future is unstable.

Numerous expedients can be adopted in improving the environment of such children. The feature common to all—except where the cause is primarily physical—is the attempt to establish some really strong affectionate relationship with an adult who loves and understands children but still realises the importance of avoiding taking the place of a parent whose outlook has to be reformed. Such a child must be made to feel that he really matters to someone; and he must be encouraged.

Sometimes all that is required is a change of school on the advice of the educational psychologist. In other cases he can be transferred for a time to a small remedial class under a teacher specially selected for her gifts of insight and affection. In other cases again he can continue to attend his ordinary school while receiving treatment at a Child Guidance Clinic. Some Local Education Authorities have established day special schools for maladjusted children; others board them out with understanding foster-parents from whose home they go to school in the ordinary way; others again maintain boarding hostels; and finally for the most difficult cases, sometimes those where the parents are unwilling or unable to co-operate or have wilfully rejected the child, there are country boarding-schools.

It is too early yet to estimate the size of the problem of maladjustment or what success the measures which are now being taken to cope with it may ultimately have in the reduction of juvenile delinquency at the one extreme and the need for mental hospital beds at the other. As any social worker or magistrate knows, however, there still remain in every area too many possible breeding-grounds—not always slums—and no one who recalls that one-third of the beds in public hospitals are still beds for the mentally sick, who looks into the present divorce and separation rate or who examines the statistics of children who have to be taken into the care of the local authorities, will be bold enough to suggest that daylight is yet discernible at the end of the tunnel.

Little need be said of the last and latest recruit to the list of those handicaps of which Local Education Authorities are now required to take cognizance, namely *speech defects*. To stammer or stutter is a real agony to the child so afflicted. It is a healthy sign of the amount which has been achieved by health education in the past 20 years that it has become bad form in most parts of the country to laugh at such a child. Equally it is far more commonly realised than was the case some years ago that the worst possible form of treatment is the quack remedy. Surprisingly there was no noticeable increase in stammering as a result of the 170,000 tons of bombs which the Germans claim to have dropped on this country during the war—or the 76,000 tons to which we admit. Those in the best position to form an opinion do not believe that there is any increase in speech defects and 49,000 children received treatment in 1,101 School Clinics from 334 speech therapists on the staff of the School Health Service in 1957.

No one who started his official life 35 years ago as a very junior member of Sir George Newman's staff in the Medical

Branch of the Board of Education can fail to recognise that we are an immeasurably finer, fitter and better-educated population. It is true that, by the very nature of the service they are giving, magistrates, heads of schools and social workers are still too often appalled that children can even in these days be found to be living here and there in such harrowing housing conditions or exposed to so much human frailty. Nevertheless all would probably admit that the attack on 'want, disease, ignorance, squalor and idleness' has been worthily begun. The truth is that the Welfare State has brought the families who used to be referred to as 'the submerged tenth' into the concentrated light of public concern and attention.

It would be a brave man, however, who felt able to be equally optimistic about the extent to which spiritual and moral advance has kept pace with mental, physical and material improvement.

Perhaps there is no more insidious mood into which the student of social legislation can allow himself to be lulled or led than the belief that we have only to implement fully the Education Act of 1944 and those other great Acts which ushered in the Welfare State to find that in some way society has been spiritually and morally regenerated in the process of mental and physical improvement and the diffusion of a more equitable standard of life.

Social advance *can* be religion in action, but only in so far as those who seek to bring it about seek to bring about simultaneously a higher *quality* of life.

PART 2
The National System

V

FUNDAMENTAL STATISTICS, PROGRESS AND FINANCE

THE STATISTICS OF PUBLIC EDUCATION IN ENGLAND AND WALES. THE STATISTICAL CHANCES THAT ANY GIVEN CHILD WILL ATTAIN TO ANY PARTICULAR TYPE OF EDUCATION. HAS THERE BEEN PROGRESS IN BRITISH EDUCATION? A BACKWARD GLANCE. HOW THE ENGLISHMAN PAYS FOR HIS CHILDREN'S EDUCATION

THE best way to obtain a picture of any properly documented educational system is, quite literally, to draw one.

Anyone with a sheet of graph paper and the statistics published in the Annual Report of the Ministry of Education can do this for England and Wales quite easily. He will find that after a few hours' work he will have produced the diagram shown as a frontispiece to this book. If he then takes a few coloured chalks and colours it he will have a picture showing exactly what an aerial colour photograph of all the 9,900,000 children, pupils and students in the schools, colleges of technology, universities, Teachers' Training Colleges and evening institutes of England and Wales would look like from about 30,000 feet. He must imagine that they have been arranged on Salisbury Plain age group by age group in squares of ten thousand holding flags above their heads coloured according to the type of school, technical college, or university attended by each. Incidentally even if they were allowed no more than one square yard apiece they would cover three square miles.

This method of delineating an educational system was originated in a Polish publication about 1930. It remains the ideal method of avoiding the constant reiteration of figures which can all too easily kill any attempt to write about public education. It can also be used to obtain some comparison of the public educational provision of one country as against that of another and this often yields surprising results.

A broad picture of national education which shows the inter-relationship of its various parts can be just as valuable to anyone who wishes to understand it as the skeleton and the diagram of the human body to the medical student. Later as a Harley Street specialist he may produce admirable disquisitions on the Thalamus, or Disdiadokakinesia in alcoholics, but he must first learn his anatomy. Even the artist or sculptor must be able to draw or model the human body before he can take liberties with it to secure an effect.

Such a graph will, too, dispel at a glance many popular illusions and misconceptions. It can equally well be constructed to show the public system of education as a whole or as it has developed in any particular area of the country. Its preparation will produce many surprises, even for the experienced educational administrator. It will reveal for example that formal education does not by any means cease, even for a majority of children, at the end of the term in which their fifteenth birthday occurs. This fact is, of course, clearly illustrated by the Table on page 76. It will show that, statistically at least, the much discussed 'Public Schools' occupy a very small area indeed in the total picture. Again it will be noticed that there is no longer any substantial number of children attending places of learning outside those provided or mainly financed by public funds. It can be seen at a glance that a respectable highway and not a narrow 'scholarship ladder' now leads to University and Higher Technological Education.

Anyone, therefore, who is called upon to speak with any frequency about public education ought to have some such visual picture of the statistical background of his subject in his mind's eye. It is even more important that he should do so where he wishes to write about the nation's schools. Many arguments about education would break down or change direction before they had been fairly launched if those taking part could be persuaded to put to themselves the awkward questions 'What are the facts?' or 'Precisely how important numerically against

STATISTICS, PROGRESS AND FINANCE

the educational background as a whole is the type of school or teaching about which I am becoming so eloquent?'

It may therefore be helpful in clarifying the statistical picture of English education today if the reader will first imagine himself in the position of the parent of, say, a child of two, a child of five, a child of eleven and a pupil reaching the end of his or her period of secondary education. He can then ask himself what arithmetically are the chances that his offspring will attain to any particular form of education.

It is improbable that there will be a place for the toddler of two in a school within the public system of education. The probability is that he will have to wait until the term in which his fifth birthday occurs. The annual intake to the nursery schools for children aged two to five at present only allows the admission each year of about one child in 65. Inevitably, and quite properly, these places usually tend to go to young children who cannot be adequately cared for otherwise during the daytime. The young children of widows, widowers, women who have been deserted by their husbands and must go out to work, mothers who are permanent invalids, or mothers who are overburdened by trying to care for aged relatives, a sick husband, or perhaps delicate twins in a small tenement flat should clearly have first claim. If he is unfortunate enough to be blind or to have sight so defective that he is going to require education by methods not involving the use of sight he can be admitted at two to a 'Sunshine Home' for blind babies, but mercifully, as already shown, only one child in 4,000/5,000 is now blind. If he is deaf he should certainly begin nursery school education at this age, but happily only about one child in 2,000 is so deaf as to have no hearing in either ear.

At five, or just before that age, about 93 in every 100 children start their school life in a State primary school. This will be conducted by the Local Education Authority or by a Voluntary Body, such as a Church in partnership with the Local Education Authority and with very substantial aid from public funds. The other seven find their way to preparatory schools of various kinds conducted by private individuals. From these a substantial proportion drift back into the main stream before they are 11 or will be found in schools recognised as efficient though not grant-aided by the Ministry of Education. More rarely they are kept at home for a while if a parent can show that they are receiving there an education appropriate to their age from their mother, an aunt or a governess. To deprive a fit and healthy child of his birthright of mixing at school with his fellows in the same age group—in the belief that he can be 'taught' better at home—is a very questionable expedient. The wife of an over-anxious Member of Parliament who had adopted it overheard her younger daughter's comment to the elder, 'You know I never really liked that man!' The ethical perceptions of young children are sometimes surprisingly acute!

For the vast majority the tradition remains entry to school at the earliest possible age. This tradition is an old one in England and probably derives from both social and economic origins. The cotton-spinner or colliery worker of the 1890's often lived in a jerry-built back-to-back house, already perhaps in its third generation of decay or subsidence. He and his wife had learnt from their parents to regard children as an economic asset. He was probably, too, impatient, in an era of much juvenile labour and little birth-control, to see the first child of the union commence work at 10 or 11. Furthermore by the time that child was two or three years of age it was often becoming imperative to relieve the narrow home of the presence of his firstborn during part at least of the day. Perhaps there was already a still younger toddler and another baby on the way. The earliest possible start at school offered a way out. Incidentally it enabled him to salve his conscience by the comforting reflection that (as Dr. Johnson said when he heard that the boys at his old school were being caned less but learning more Greek) the child was gaining at one end what it might lose at the other!

Thus in 1895, the first year by which England and Wales could offer a school place—eight square feet of floor area—to every child up to the age of 11, there were 634,000 children under five in the schools as compared with just a third of that number today (210,622). This is a welcome indication of the improvement in the interval of housing, economic and social conditions, although the admission to school of children under five is controlled today in many areas which are short of school places.

Nevertheless, England and Wales are still almost alone among the countries of the world in requiring all children to begin their school days at five rather than six years of age. Surprisingly, too, they are still among the comparatively few countries where every child's birth has been so meticulously anticipated, registered and followed up by the health visitor and school welfare officer that none can for long evade the law. By contrast a charming test of eligibility for entry to school was often applied before the war in the Dutch East Indies where birth certificates were uncommon. 'Can you touch your left ear with your right hand over the top of your head?' A child of normal physical development who can perform this feat can be presumed to be six!

There follows a normal pattern of two to three years in the infant school and three to four in the junior school.

Shortly before a child reaches his eleventh milestone, in most parts of the country, though, as we have seen, no longer in all, his road still branches into three, the signposts reading respectively, 'To the Secondary Grammar School', 'To the Secondary Technical (or Art) School', 'To the Secondary Modern School'. Not all Local Education Authorities, however, can as yet offer the secondary technical option, and many secondary technical schools still commence at 13 years of age.

In theory the sole determinant which road any individual child ought to take is his aptitude (or bent of mind) and attainment. In practice upwards of 50% aim at first to squeeze through the narrow entrances to the first or second road. This is because as parents we nearly all want to experience a comfortable feeling that our child is going to enjoy—as we suppose—better educational opportunities than we may have enjoyed ourselves. Few parents understand that in terms of ultimate human happiness the best road for their child is likely to be that along which he can travel at his own best pace. It is certainly not the place of the educationist to moralise, however. His object should be to see that the alternative to the grammar school may not only be more suitable in theory but by its success demonstrate to parents that it is in reality more suitable in practice.

As we have seen—the elimination, by a selection test or an elaborate comparison of school records in the junior school, of the traffic jam which would otherwise be caused is a matter of much heart-burning and controversy.

Eventually about one in five[1] will pass the turnstiles into the road marked 'To the Secondary Grammar School' although there are wide differences in this proportion from area to area. Not more than one in about 25 can at present hope eventually to follow the road marked 'To the Secondary Technical School'. About 60 in 100 will continue on the road to the 'Secondary Modern School'. The balance of the age group (15%) will be distributed over the remaining schools which cater for children of all ages from 5 to 15 (20,551 out of 629,000). It is now the first objective of National Policy to eliminate these 'all age' schools. 42,000 out of 629,000 will be found in private schools outside the public system of education. A large proportion of the remainder will be in special schools for the handicapped.

What is likely to happen to the English child of today when he reaches the age of 15? Statistically the answer is fairly simple. Taking 100 such children nearly 40 will be remaining at secondary schools of various types, three or four of them at secondary technical schools and one will be in a special or hospital school for the handicapped.

The other 59 will have left school to enter Industry, Commerce, Agriculture or to help at home. This is not by any means the whole story, for at least a quarter of them will have enrolled in Evening Classes while about 16% of the boys and 5% of the girls will be in jobs where the employers are enlightened enough to be prepared to send them in working hours and without loss of pay to attend day classes related to their work, as shown by the Table on page 76. This pattern repeats itself with those who leave at 16.

Of those remaining at schools within the public system of education till 17, 18 or 19, 24 in every 100 enter Universities, 16 Teachers' Training Colleges, and probably about 20 courses of Further Education at Technical or Art Colleges or other types of Institution. The other 40 probably pass in nearly every case

---

[1] 19·07%, counting those who enter the grammar streams of bilateral, multilateral and comprehensive secondary schools and were receiving education of grammar school type at the age of 12 in January 1958.

into employment from which they would normally enter upon a course of evening studies, professional, artistic, linguistic or 'home making' in the case of the young women, but in the case of the young men usually only after they have undertaken any military service obligations.

Before passing from the statistics it may be interesting to note that by 1951–52 one young man or woman in every 32 in England, every 28 in Wales and every 27 in Scotland reached the University. 72·4% of them were assisted to do so by grants. Barely 12 years earlier the figures had been one in 63, one in 79, and one in 42 respectively and only 41·1% had been assisted. For the purpose of obtaining these figures it has had to be assumed that the three nationalities used the Universities in their own country. Unfortunately no up-to-date figures are readily available although the probability is that they have come down to about one in 25 of the age group.

By way of contrast it may be recalled that in 1888, well within the lifetime of these young people's grandfathers, Mr. T. Smythe, described as 'a representative of the working classes', was hotly protesting to a Royal Commission that 'It would be next to expecting a boy out of the London Board Schools to take wings as to expect him to advance by his own efforts to the University'. Even during their father's early life (1900) the odds against such an occurrence were probably still about 1,000 to one. Indeed it is really only by contrast that the educationist can answer the young men and women of today when they ask the question 'Has public education in Britain advanced, and if so, how rapidly?'

The student of 50 or 100 years hence who wishes to obtain a living impression of the social atmosphere and events of today will, no doubt, be able to select and view at his ease, from the comfort of an armchair, appropriate film and television records from a national library. The student of today who wishes to look back no more than the sixty years which have passed since 1900 finds it no easy task to obtain a balanced picture of the largely unco-ordinated patchwork of schools which in his grandfather's time the County Councils inherited from the School Boards on the passage of the Education Act of 1902, and to contrast them with the 'unity in diversity' which now exists.

The fact is that the process of co-ordination and improvement has taken place on so wide a front as to defy broad generalisation and yet to render detailed description both laborious for the writer and tedious for the reader.

Let us suppose by way of illustration that a visitor possessing no specialised knowledge of education could be projected back and enabled to make an inspection of, for example, 1,000 'elementary' schools as he would have found them in 1900 and a similar inspection of a further 1,000 schools of today. It is just possible that, unless his perceptions were very acute, he might carry away the impression that no change so striking as justly to be called revolutionary had taken place. About the same proportion of the buildings would be new and would no doubt be described by the teachers serving in them as containing every modern comfort. About the same proportion would mark a clear breakaway from earlier ideas of school planning. He could hardly fail to experience a greater sensation of light, space and fresh air in the schools of today, but, owing to the limitations imposed in many urban areas by site values, this impression of spaciousness would probably be very much less striking than that which would be occasioned by a similar round of visits to past and present schools in the country. A superficial study of the children might suggest to him that the schools of today seemed to have become much more homogeneous in respect of the age and intelligence of the children attending them. In the towns there would be considerably fewer school departments containing children of all ages from infants to those of 12 to 14. In the country he would still encounter too many of these; and 12 would have become 15. Next he would certainly notice that the classes seemed considerably smaller and their teachers if not considerably bigger at least of greater stature both physically and intellectually. In particular he would find no young people of 14 to 18 in charge of classes. The two or three children—sometimes more—in every class of 1900 with heavy or ragged clothing, and no boots or very inadequate boots, the two or three obviously of very low intelligence, often to the point of mental defect, the two or three obviously shortsighted, pallid or ill would have been spirited away. Speech and looks, too, would obviously have improved. There would be more unoccupied classrooms. If our visitor inquired the reason he would probably discover that the opportunities for practical work, no longer invariably taken in a distant 'centre' but usually on the school site itself, had enormously increased. On further inquiry he would learn that classes were out of school on visits to swimming-baths, the public library, the docks, a museum; others might be spending a day at a playing field some distance away. Others again might be enjoying a fortnight at a school camp far away in the country or even travelling on the Continent on a school journey.

It is to be hoped that he would remark the absence today of sing-song repetition of multiplication tables or lists of words, countries, capes and islands. He might notice that in the schools of 1900 all the children in a class had seemed, all too often, to be doing precisely the same thing at the same moment. All would have been only too ready to regard him on his entry with eyes part curious, part furtive. By contrast every individual in many classrooms today would be occupied either in small groups or in some separate pursuit and would often be far too engrossed in it to look up.

Repeatedly in his round of visits to the schools of 1960 he would come upon classes engaged in a debate, rehearsing a play, watching a puppet theatre, constructing a historical or geographical model, drinking their mid-morning milk, listening to a musical appreciation lesson, or watching an educational film, or school television lesson. He would encounter school orchestras at practice, apparatus work in progress in school gymnasia, vigorous games of netball between teams clad in the lightest of clothing who could look forward to a shower-bath after the game. Looking back he would probably wonder why such things seemed to be missing from his impressions of the schools of 1900 and only be able to recall an occasional maypole or a class here and there handling specimens from a school 'museum cupboard' or measuring the area of the playground as part of a practical arithmetic lesson. He might wonder, too, what had happened to the formal massed drills in boots and heavy clothing, and what had happened to the schools where 'wrist and arm' drill (each pupil standing at or on his desk) had, in the absence of any playground at all, been the sole physical training possible. He would observe how an engaging friendliness between teacher and pupil seemed to have replaced the rather stiff and formal relations of the past as completely as the tunic or light frock has replaced the pinafore and the soft collar and shorts the hard, but often far from clean, 'Eton' collar or muffler and corduroys. It is unlikely that any teacher of the 1900 era would explain to him, as one did to a Royal Commission: 'We have to avoid moving about among the children too much because, even though I have sewn bags of sulphur round the hem of my skirt, the fleas and bugs still get up!' Certainly none would be so immodest as to explain that her skirt must touch the ground at the back lest in bending over a child a male colleague should see her ankles! He would notice, perhaps, that books seemed far more plentiful, better written, better illustrated, cleaner and less formal. He would make a mental note that apparatus seemed to be more abundant, ranging from wheeled toys, shop counters and 'Wendy' houses in the infants' departments to physics and chemistry apparatus, ordnance and relief maps, biological aquaria, spinning-wheels and hand looms for the senior children. He would be attracted by pleasantly framed pictures ranging from gay 'moderns' with a leavening of original works by rising artists and selected children to reproductions of the world's masterpieces in colour. He could hardly fail to contrast these with the oleographs of Queen Victoria and steel engravings of highland cattle in the schools of 1900 or to note that picture-making on paper had replaced geometrical scratchings on slates. If he was interested in hygiene he would be relieved to find that where he had noticed one towel spreading infection among 400 boys, there is now usually an automatic towel cabinet or a hand towel for each with a sufficient supply of soap and usually hot water as well as cold.

But if—as is quite possible—his imagination did not at first force him to recognise in all these things the symbols of that revolution in the nation's schools which has crept silently forward for nearly a century, he should be acquitted of any apparent want of perception. The individual who can witness change and appreciate in a flash the administrative effort, the years of planning and training, the frustrations and disappointments, the millions of money which have gone to its creation, is a very rare individual indeed. More rarely still can he realise how slowly changes reflect themselves in the human material which they influence.

Despite many claims put forward by this country or that to have revolutionised their educational system within a decade, educational systems which are both well found and broadly based are not brought into existence overnight.

If we are shown photographs we can all of us perhaps see change as between the individual child of today and his prototype of 1900. Some of us can see it as applied to a whole class of children, perhaps even to a whole school. But few of us have the width of vision to grasp what it has meant to provide the whole sum of the separate items which have gone to the production of those changes in order that they may permeate and revivify schools attended by six and a half millions of the nation's children. For six million children marching 12 abreast would stretch the 300 miles from London to Newcastle or would take nearly three weeks to count at 200 a minute!

The modern democratic ideal postulates, moreover, that every single child in this vast procession must be afforded the individual attention of a trained teacher every day. Only one will be Britain's Prime Minister in the year 2000, but every individual may be tomorrow's banner headline and may bring about the end of some teacher's or educational administrator's professional career!

Some of the more striking differences—for example those in the physique, behaviour, clothing, or facial appearance of the children—would no doubt be attributed by sociologists to broad social trends other than those directly brought about by the educational work and influence of Local Education Authorities and the teaching profession backed by enlightened School Medical and Dental services. They would be placed to the credit, for example, of improved housing. They would be attributed to the growth *pari passu* with public medical, dental and nursing services of a national health conscience. Other sociologists would quite rightly point to the diffusion of wealth brought about by trade unionism, the increased opportunities for the exercise of thrift by the small investor and broad economic changes in industry and commerce. The social historian would remind us of the substitution of ready-made and mass-produced clothing for bespoke tailored garments (which so often passed from the mansion to the slum through the second-hand shop, the pawn-broker's establishment and finally the street barrow). Those interested in culture and the Arts would point to the broad cultural influence increasingly exercised in recent years by the cinemas, broadcasting and television.

Yet it is tempting to see, as the primary social and cultural force permeating and sustaining the whole, the influences and ideals which have surrounded every citizen of the future during his school days: to recall that they have surrounded him, too, a little more effectively and for a little longer in each generation. It seems indisputable, if one takes a long enough view of social progress, that the schools must, however slowly, be raising, in each generation that passes through them, the standards of community consciousness, hygiene and mental alertness. Clearly, too, public education has had much to do with the improvement in the national capacity for combination and ability to avoid thoughtless extravagance or uneconomic waste.

If our visitor to the schools of 1900 and 1960 were to inquire what were the six or seven principal ways in which the Local Education Authorities have contributed directly to this process, probably no two persons engaged in the educational services would supply him with the same list.

A social historian untrammelled by preconceived theories as to the relative importance of different facets of the educational services might single out the following:

(1) The steps taken by the State as represented by the Board (and later Ministry) of Education in partnership with the Local Authorities and the teachers' professional bodies since 1900 to raise teaching power. This has involved the progressive improvement of the educational qualifications of the teaching staff. To achieve this it has been necessary to attract the best educational

material available each year into the Training Colleges through salary and similar inducements. Without encouragement of initiative and the creation in the individual teacher's mind of that sense of freedom, in the absence of which initiative cannot be exercised, much good material might have run to waste. Again, without a recognition that merit alone will ensure promotion a number of the best teachers might have left the profession. Facilities for all teachers to keep up to date through such media as refresher courses and teachers' libraries have played an important part. Finally a steady expansion of the number of teachers employed, thus rendering possible a progressive reduction in the size of classes, has been of paramount importance.

(2) The linking of the system of primary education, at first through scholarships and fees representing considerably less than the full cost, with an expanding system of secondary grammar schools. The concurrent creation of alternatives to grammar school education through secondary technical schools and specialist courses at the top of secondary modern schools has been an important corollary. Since the passage of the Education Act of 1944 there has been steadily expanding effort to create an appropriate secondary education for all through the improvement of the old senior elementary schools and their revivification into up-to-date modern schools.

(3) The enlightened policy followed by so many of the Local Education Authorities in the important matter of educational 'plant'. This has not stopped short at the provision of actual school buildings but has spread outwards to cover the humbler but no less essential supply of books, apparatus, materials, livestock and pets, lantern slides, clothing, apparatus for visual education, games and modern physical training.

(4) The solicitude displayed by all Local Education Authorities in their dealings with the delicate or tubercular child, with those handicapped by blindness, mental defect, deafness and crippling conditions, with the child unable to obtain full benefit from school attendance by reason of lack of food, boots and clothing or the conditions of its home.

(5) The equality of treatment accorded to the schools, whether primary or secondary, provided by bodies other than the Local

Authorities with that accorded to schools provided by the Local Authority itself.

(6) The orderly advance, on the broadest front compatible with proper financial control and planning, achieved through the system of triennial 'programmes' and capital investment.

How does the ordinary Englishman pay for the education of his children? To answer this question it is not necessary, as is too often supposed, to prepare oneself for an expedition into the arid desert of Central and Local Government finance. Reduced to its simplest terms the answer is that we all—every single one of us—pay, in part continuously, in part by very moderate six-monthly instalments spread over our whole working lives, for the cost not only of our own children's schooling but often for that of our nephews, nieces and grandchildren as well. The actual amount we pay is determined locally by the size, amenity and character of the house and garden we occupy. Nationally it depends upon the size of our income and the amount of our expenditure on food, drink, tobacco, entertainment and other commodities taxed by the Central Government.

Let us take one or two simple illustrations:

Mr. and Mrs. Average on marriage when the husband is 26 succeed in obtaining a Council house or flat provided by the Local Authority and assessed by that same Authority at the current average rateable value of £26 10s. a year. The self-same Local Authority, this time in its capacity not as Housing Authority but as Education Authority, finds that, after grants in aid from the Central Government, paid through the Ministry of Education, have been allowed for, it will still be necessary to levy a rate of 6s. 7½d. on every £1 of rateable value to meet the local rate-borne share of the cost of its schools.

On their £26 10s. rateable value Mr. and Mrs. Average will, therefore, have to pay 6s. 7½d. multiplied by 26·5—roughly 3s. a week or £7 15s. a year.

Their scale of living is humble, they never achieve a larger and therefore more highly rated dwelling, and have only one child, who, however, rewards them by being intelligent enough to be kept on at secondary school till 18 to secure a good pass in the

General Certificate of Education at Advanced Level. The cost of educating this child to the Central Government and the Local Authority respectively will (at 1958-59 costs) be £970 made up as follows:

	Government Grants	Local Authority Rates	Total
Six years' primary education	£210	£80	£290
Four years' secondary education to 15	£198	£92	£290
Three years' secondary education to 18	£252	£138	£390
Total	£660	£310	£970

During these 13 years Mr. Average will not, of course, have contributed through his smoking and visits to the cinema or the public house the £660 which his child's education has cost the taxpayer. Towards the £310 which it has cost the local ratepayer he will have contributed 13 × £7 15s., namely £100 15s. But in the years between his marriage and that in which his child enters school and the years of life which he enjoys after the child leaves school (before dying as he must unfortunately for the purpose of this life story be made to do at 66, since that is the average expectation of life for a man) he will have paid 27 more sums of £7 15s., namely £209 5s. Adding this to the £100 15s. which, it will be remembered, he paid during his child's 13 years at school, we find that he has, in fact, during his 40 years' tenure of his modest dwelling exactly paid back the £310 which the 13 years' education cost him and his fellow ratepayers. Five cigarettes a day and a very modest couple of pints of beer every week will pay back the Exchequer contribution of £660 over the same 40 years.

As with Mr. and Mrs. Average, so with Mr. and Mrs. Commuter, who occupy a pleasant house in a suburb assessed for rates at £55. In their 40 years of married life they will pay £620 in education rate at 6s. 7½d. or nearly the cost of educating four children to the age of 15, or two till 18.

Mr. and Mrs. Richman, on the other hand, who achieve the pinnacle of their ambitions at the 'Turrets' rated at £300 a year, may, if they ever make the calculation, find that they have, in addition to spending the price of a Rolls-Royce on the education at private boarding-schools of their son and daughter, provided the rate-borne cost of roughly 20 children attending the local school from 5 to 15.

These figures bring out clearly a fact which is as yet little appreciated. The respective proportions of the total national expenditure on education borne by the local rates and the central Exchequer taxation have changed greatly as compared with pre-war years. This can best be appreciated by an examination of the following figures:

Year 1938–39			*Year 1958–59*		
Total Exchequer and Rates	£97·4 million		£613·2 million		Total Exchequer and Rates
Divided Exchequer	£49·1	,,	£389·3	,,	Exchequer
Rates, etc.	£48·3	,,	£223·9	,,	Rates, etc.

The £97·4 million of 1938–39 represented 1·9% of the gross national product. The £613 million of 1958–59 about 3·0% of the estimated gross national product.

The £49·1 million Exchequer contribution in 1938–39 represented about 5·2% of the total ordinary Exchequer expenditure of the United Kingdom. The £389 million Exchequer contribution of 1958–59 represented 5·22% of the total Exchequer expenditure on current and capital account in 1958.

VI

PROGRESS WITH THE REPLACEMENT OF FIRST-GENERATION SCHOOL BUILDINGS AND THE EXPANSION OF THE TEACHING FORCE

WHAT PROPORTION OF OUR SCHOOL BUILDINGS ARE SERIOUSLY OUT OF DATE? CRITICS OF THE PACE OF OUR EDUCATIONAL BUILDING PROGRAMMES SHOULD BEWARE OF USING PRE-WAR ARGUMENTS. OUR PROBLEMS COMPARED WITH THOSE OF THE UNITED STATES. THE PROBLEM OF SECURING ENOUGH TEACHERS FOR THE INCREASE IN SCHOOL ROLLS SINCE 1943. OUR PRECIOUS RESERVES OF HIGHLY TRAINED MAN AND WOMAN POWER.

OUR propensity for disparaging or minimising our national achievements is often remarkable. Fortunately this is at last becoming recognised by some of our friends abroad. They are in fact now tending, in increasing numbers, to drop in on us by air or sea to look for the facts behind our smoke-screen of deprecatory understatement. It has, however, perhaps tended to obscure what was achieved between the wars in replacing our oldest schools. There is still, for example, quite a widespread belief among those who derive their impressions of English education exclusively from newspaper articles and the Jeremiads of educational conferences, or even those of Parliamentary Committees, that 80% or 90% of our school accommodation was built before the 20th century opened; and that it has been allowed ever since to become more and more out of date, if not structurally dilapidated, with every year.

Anyone, however, who subscribes and seeks to attain to the definition of an educated man or woman as one in whose presence one hesitates to enter into an argument without a basis of fact to support one's assertions, will do well to regard such sweeping assumptions with some suspicion.

Unfortunately in this instance it is not particularly easy to arrive at the full and precise facts.

Those who take the trouble to look up the Housing statistics of the Ministry of Health for the years between the wars can soon discover—though it will probably surprise them—that alone among the countries of the civilized world our prodigious housing effort during those years succeeded, after a painfully slow start amounting to only 5,000 new houses in the first two years, in re-housing one-third of the population (14,000,000 people). Indeed it was this achievement which alone served to render endurable not only the Government evacuation scheme of Hitler's war but the infinitely greater wartime reshuffle of population due to the mobilization of industry which witnessed 60 million moves of individuals from one area to another. The small team who took part before war broke out in the planning of evacuation and knew the comparable housing statistics for Germany could appreciate what in fact lay behind Marshal Goering's repeated boast that Germany had no need of such a scheme!

Anyone, however, who goes on to ask the apparently straightforward question how many new school places were provided in those same years to serve the new housing estates and the large-scale movement of industries such as for example the growth between the wars of the South Yorks coalfield, where the birth-rate rose to 33 per 1,000, will look in vain for an answer.

An analysis of the Annual Reports of the Board of Education between such vital years of reorganisation as those from 1926–39 might suggest that the officials who compiled them were interested first and foremost in the elimination of a number of comparatively small schools, attended by a relatively small percentage of the school population, which His Majesty's Inspectors had placed on a 'Black List'. Politically, it is true these schools were a thorn in the flesh but the reports pass over almost unnoticed the incomparably more important building programmes which were providing a new place in a new school for nearly every child who moved with his parents to, or was born in, one of the new housing areas; and were reconditioning a large proportion of the oldest schools to provide for smaller numbers.

All that can be discovered, by a somewhat extensive process of extraction and cross-reference from a pile of blue books, is that in actual fact during these years a respectable total of 1,800 new primary and senior elementary schools and 120 secondary grammar schools were built and opened; and that an even more respectable total of 10,235 schools, representing just half the number of schools then existing in England and Wales, were enlarged, remodelled, reconditioned or improved.

Probably the great majority of these 1,800 new schools were large and virtually all of them would be planned on the basis of primary education ending and a completely new stage of senior (or secondary) education beginning at the age of 11. This had in fact been the central recommendation of the Hadow Report of 1926 on 'The Education of the Adolescent'. The average size of the 84 schools built in Wales is ascertainable, namely 430. This would suggest that something like 825,000 places were provided in new schools and perhaps a round million after adding the places provided by enlargements.[1] This is borne out by the capital expenditure sanctioned during these years, namely £66,500,00. For in those halcyon days of low labour costs and ready availability of traditional building materials a primary school place could normally be provided for about £35 and a place in a senior school for about £65. There are already fortunate areas in the country where 70% of the schools are under 30 years old. Indeed it is probably a fair assumption that but for the war we should by 1954 have completed the reorganisation of our whole school system into separate primary and secondary schools and virtually rebuilt or remodelled every school dating from the pre-1926 era.

The educational building machine was in fact by 1938 accelerating smoothly in top gear. If capital expenditure and building costs had remained stationary at the 1938–39 level, a further £230,000,000 would have been spent by 1954. Such a

[1] Professor R. M. Titmuss, *Problems of Social Policy*, p. 407, arrives at a figure of a million new school places provided between 1919 and 1945 after allowing for 10% war losses, using a different method of compilation.

sum would have been amply sufficient but for the economic and price changes and the destruction caused by the war.

At this point it might be advisable to illustrate the marked difference in the arguments available to anyone who wishes to set himself up today as a knowledgeable critic of the pace of the country's educational building programme as compared with those available to his pre-war prototype.

'Knowledgeable' is the operative word because the contrast between our pre-war and post-war economy in the matter of building labour and capital investment often seems to be imperfectly understood by those who speak or write on the subject. Before the war the market for building labour was to a large extent a free market. The critic on his way to visit, or perhaps teach in, some antediluvian school would pass the super cinema going up at the street corner, skirt round the barrows of the local builders' workmen erecting a new façade to the multiple shop, knock his head on the scaffolding outside the pin-table saloon. He might well arrive at his school saying in effect: 'Every concern in this town seems to be able to find the money and labour for luxury building: yet the Town Council tell us that they cannot afford to bring their educational plant up to date.'

In a sense this would have been less than fair. Firstly because a great deal of educational building, remodelling and enlargement had in fact, as shown above, taken place between 1926 and 1938. Secondly because by 1938, in an effort to prepare for the raising of the school-leaving age, due to take place on the day war actually commenced, the nation was in fact spending £16½ million in that year on its schools. This £16½ million represented 5·5% of the £300 million which was being devoted in that year's public building programme to capital equipment such as houses and public buildings, new electricity stations and gasworks, factories, roads, railway tracks, locomotives and rolling-stock. Educational building was probably in fact absorbing about 6% of the total building labour employed on this £300 million programme, for the brick-built schools with wooden floors of 1938 consumed more man hours of strictly building labour than is the case with modern school design and constructional methods. Nevertheless it cannot have been absorbing more than 3% to 4%

of the total labour force in the building industry after taking into account those engaged in the free market for private building.

When the war came it very soon became a paramount necessity to divert every available unit of man (and eventually woman) power and every available ounce of materials, even those required for repair, to the national war effort. A large part of those overseas assets, which formed such an important item in our invisible exports, had to be sold and our capital stock was run down, by under-maintenance, perhaps to the tune of £300 million a year. A fifth of our schools were destroyed or damaged, a percentage which may have been roughly paralleled in the case of our pre-war factories and similar capital assets. More than half our pre-war merchant tonnage was sunk, 222,000 houses were completely destroyed out of a probable total of 3,745,000 *different* houses destroyed or damaged, or nearly two houses in every seven. The end of hostilities found us with a total building labour force much reduced from its pre-war total; 6,000,000 workers to be diverted from the Services and war production to peace production; an immediate need for at least a million new houses to enable a separate home to be offered to each family who wanted one; virtually the whole of our pre-war capital plant crying out for repair and re-equipment; and an imperative demand for new factories to set our export trade on its feet again.

Thus although in the realm of ideas the effect of the war had been to advance by 15 years the popular demand for a public system of education genuinely capable of serving a classless democracy, in the realm of hard facts it had retarded by at least 20 years the possibility of the substantial realisation of any such ideal!

The schools which had been destroyed had to be rebuilt, those which had been damaged repaired. Bricked-up windows and playground shelters had to be cleared. Kitchens and dining-rooms were needed to enable a start to be made with the daily dinner at school promised as part of the social security programme. A considerably greater number of places than those actually lost by bombing needed to be written off to reduce the size of classes to a more realistic level. Class-rooms designed for 50 infants or juniors at 10 square feet of floor space per child or

40 seniors at 12 square feet had for example to be written down to 40 juniors at 12½ square feet or 30 of secondary age at 16 square feet.

Moreover, not only were there acute shortages in all the traditional building materials but the capacity of the industry which, after revaluation to pre-war values, should have been £1,200 million a year was found to have declined to £700 million.

The raising of the school-leaving age to 15, a reform long overdue, would require school places to be found for another age group of 320,000 children.[1] Lastly, overshadowing the whole educational scene and upsetting every calculation of those whose planning might still tend to run in a pre-war groove, came the astonishing upsurge in the birth-rate, which has continued in every year from 1943 onwards, known in educational circles as the 'bulge'. Local education authorities found that by 1958 they would be confronted with 1,800,000 more children in school than at the end of the war. Had they known it this would become 2,059,000 more by 1958 owing largely to voluntary lengthening of school life. Clearly the supply of new teachers every year to replace wastage and increase the total must be more than doubled. Added to this a minimum of £50 million must be found for higher technical education.

Such a concatenation of unpredictable difficulties would probably have proved a challenge utterly beyond the executive capacity of the Board of Education as it was constituted after the First World War. For in those days it resembled a charmingly erudite University Senior Common Room. Moreover the administrative machine in the local education offices was in those far-off days, to say the least of it, hardly impressive. Fortunately both at Government and County level a new generation of administrators with a much wider vision had, under the hard necessity of total war, developed a capacity for large-scale administrative organisation and executive planning which was able to rise to the occasion.

Through the generosity—too readily forgotten—of the United States and Canada in making loans to us we were able in the two years between the end of the war and December 1947

[1] The rest of the age group were already staying on at school voluntarily.

to make a net investment in home industry, houses and public utilities, including schools, of £1,300–£1,400 million.

Of this great sum, however, in the jostle for priorities, the provision of schools, technical colleges and school meals centres had only accounted for an amount of £52·2 million approved (3·73% of the total) and £17 million completed (1·22% of the total).

Let us at this point return to our critic. He is still making his way to his antediluvian school. It is nearly 10 years older and looks 20. The black-out has been taken down, the windows reglazed and the shelters which occupied so much of the playground space have been removed—only however to be replaced by a large hut used as a school dining centre and kitchen. Its classrooms are rather overcrowded with the overflow children from the new housing estate. On his way our critic has had to avoid the bicycles turning into the new export factory, and step warily over the tramlines which were being taken up as part of the steel recovery programme. 'Why in Heaven's name,' he would ask, 'should only 3·73% of the total capital programme of the past two years have gone into new educational building? We could afford to put 5·5% of our pre-war annual capital equipment programme into such building.'

It was a fair question but there was this substantial difference as compared with 1938. Building was no longer a free market. The cinemas, shop-fronts and pin-table saloons had no place in it. Every pound available for capital investment and every unit of the building labour force had been rationed and must be competed for in what the outsider's imagination saw as a cut-throat game of poker between the Whitehall Departments with the Ministry of Works holding the chips and the Treasury acting as banker in the background.

Criticism to be effective had therefore to proceed along one of two lines. Either the critic must be prepared to prove that the total sum made available annually for capital investment was insufficient—and he needed to be a very competent economist indeed to follow this difficult path through the intricacies of dollar resources, exports, imports and defence expenditure. Or he must discover precisely how much capital investment and how much building labour had been allotted by the Government to each Department, what each was spending it on and then balance the totals and priorities against the total allotted to educational building.

For example, he had to ask himself, should new housing and the new towns take priority over the rebuilding of an old school —provided of course new schools had been built to serve the new houses? How large a slice of the cake had been allotted to export industries and where did they come as compared with rebuilding schools? What proportion had gone to the development of Atomic power stations, to our 750,000 farmers and landowners in the drive to keep farm output up to wartime levels? What had the nation found it imperative to spend on new electricity generating plants and gasworks, or bringing the coal industry up to date and developing open-cast mining? How far had the needs of Civil Aviation been met and were we building any new or reconditioning any old hospitals, police stations, fire stations, prisons, post offices? Had transport fared better than Education, or new roads, or the housing of the Defence Services? It was in fact much easier to form an approximate idea of the annual sum which everyone in the world of public education would have liked to see the Minister win in the game of poker than to decide what one would have liked his fellow players to go without if he won such a sum!

Immediately after the war, a Committee on School Sites and Buildings Procedure under the Chairmanship of Mr. (later Sir William) Cleary, then Deputy Secretary of the Ministry of Education, examined how much it would cost to implement fully the 'Development Plans' and 'Further Education Schemes' of local education authorities; in other words, to bring our whole educational plant up to date and so begin to fulfil the Education Act of 1944.

They found that a sum of £1,000 million would be required: and they expressed the opinion that, on the assumption that at least double the amount of building labour employed on educational building in 1938 could be obtained, this goal could be achieved in 15 years for an annual expenditure of £70 million.

It may therefore be worth while to examine how far short

of this aspiration we have in fact fallen in the 15-year period in the face of mounting building costs and successive economy campaigns. These have at times given the capital investment Inter-Departmental 'poker game' more the character of a game of 'snakes and ladders'.

The White Paper on Capital Investment 1948 (Cmd 7268) was probably the first official publication which enabled the ordinary citizen to get a broad picture of the proportion of the total national capital investment allotted to the public system of education and to compare it with the other demands which had to be met.

For succeeding years no exactly comparable figures are available. It is, however, possible to get some idea of them from a table (No. 60) published in the National Income and Expenditure Blue Book. This table shows the gross fixed capital formation each year from 1948 to 1959. The education figures will cover not only building but total outlay including equipment, machinery and vehicles. It will moreover include, without showing separately, capital expenditure by Universities and independent schools and will cover England, Wales and Scotland.

When summarized under headings this table supplies a most illuminating picture of the broad front upon which England has been re-equipping her competitive capacity since the war.

It is essential to recall the breadth of this front before one criticises the apparent slowness of advance on any particular sector of it, still more so before one is tempted to compare Britain's performance on the educational sector with that of another country where the facts of economic life may be entirely different. For example Northern Ireland reorganised and substantially rebuilt her educational system with great rapidity after her Education Act of 1947, but she had built up substantial credits in Britain during the years of war and was still enjoying comparative economic prosperity. Moreover the total number of children in her schools is barely half that in the schools of the London County Council.

It is not possible in a book of this size and scope to do more than present the reader with the material from which he may draw his own conclusions. It will be observed, however, that the slice of the national investment cake allotted to education and child care (the latter accounting for an insignificant portion of the total) over the eleven years covered when added to that made available in 1946 and 1947 totalled roughly £950 million for buildings and equipment, £840 million for building alone. When the 1959 figures become available the total will thus have topped the £1,000 million.

Again, as the following figures show, the proportion of the total national investment in buildings and site works, and therefore of the total national building labour force available, allotted to education tended to fall off during the three years 1952, 1953 and 1954 as the national housing effort reached its peak, but it has subsequently recovered.

PROPORTION OF TOTAL CAPITAL INVESTMENT IN BUILDING ALLOTTED TO EDUCATION

1948	1949	1950	1951	1952	1953	1954	1955	1956	1957	1958
As proportion of total for all services											
4·43%	5·73%	6·83%	7·35%	6·80%	5·98%	5·91%	6·06%	6·94%	7·95%	8·0%
As proportion of total for social services											
7·50%	10·44%	13·00%	13·55%	11·93%	9·89%	10·06%	11·36%	13·69%	16·36%	17·73%

These figures do not, unfortunately, indicate that we are now very near the goal set by the Cleary Committee as those required to implement the 'Development Plans' and 'Further Education Schemes' prepared by local education authorities under the Education Act 1944. Educational horizons always recede and it will probably be 1965 before we do so unless capital investment in housing is allowed to fall off more sharply. Certainly education has fared very much more favourably than the health services where at the present rate of capital investment it would take 200 years before our present hospitals are replaced.

The mathematically inclined will be tempted to re-evaluate the figures in terms of pre-war values. So far as the total expenditure on maintaining the educational service is concerned this is a fair exercise and yields the surprising result that England and Wales was spending more on public education in 1921 than in 1948 and more in 1938 than in the early post-war years.

GROSS FIXED CAPITAL FORMATION (in £ millions)

	1948 T	1948 B	1949 T	1949 B	1950 T	1950 B	1951 T	1951 B	1952 T	1952 B	1953 T	1953 B	1954 T	1954 B	1955 T	1955 B	1956 T	1956 B	1957 T	1957 B	1958 T	1958 B
Social Services:																						
(1) Housing		337		332		331		376		494		630		644		614		626		619		581
(2) Education and child care	30	28	44	40	58	51	69	61	78	69	80	71	82	74	90	81	113	102	137	125	145	130
(3) Health Services	16	7	20	10	20	10	22	11	22	13	23	13	25	15	27	15	28	14	34	17	35	19
(4) National Assistance	1	1	1	1	2	1	2	2	2	2	2	2	3	2	3	3	3	3	3	3	4	3
Total		373		383		393		450		578		716		735		713		745		764		733
Public Services:																						
(1) Roads and public lighting, sewerage and land drainage	43	36	45	37	54	44	70	54	72	59	80	69	81	70	77	75	104	89	108	94	100	96
(2) Electricity	99	25	122	33	138	36	149	36	159	37	180	41	214	50	247	48	246	47	265	56	295	66
(3) Gas and water	39	19	49	27	57	31	68	38	80	46	85	51	89	54	95	58	92	60	92	60	89	57
(4) Other public services	24	18	21	14	27	18	35	22	29	18	26	17	26	17	29	20	33	21	31	20	31	22
Transport Services:																						
(1) Railways	40	10	42	11	44	9	44	8	40	10	54	12	63	9	69	9	90	16	127	31	140	44
(2) Road passenger	37	3	44	4	41	4	30	4	28	6	23	4	25	4	21	3	24	4	22	3	23	4
(3) Shipping	78	—	70	1	64	1	53	—	53	1	83	1	81	1	75	1	101	1	128	1	145	2
(4) Air	12	3	17	4	14	5	12	4	13	4	16	6	16	5	25	5	33	5	57	8	48	8
(5) Harbours, Docks and Canals	7	5	8	6	9	7	10	7	11	7	13	7	13	7	12	7	15	8	17	11	20	13
(6) Postal, telephone, and radio communications	37	2	43	3	44	3	52	4	63	5	71	6	76	6	87	6	97	8	102	11	91	11
Agriculture, Forestry and Fishing	94	21	94	23	93	22	95	22	97	20	94	23	101	24	111	26	103	28	120	27	118	29
Coal Mining and Quarrying	28	6	35	7	32	8	34	11	46	15	52	21	79	27	77	30	92	34	100	36	106	39
Building and Contracting Distribution services. Road goods transport	20	2	22	2	23	3	32	4	37	4	37	5	40	5	50	12	47	10	53	11	57	10
Manufacturing industries	145	27	174	48	191	61	211	64	221	73	242	77	304	101	393	131	427	169	454	193	549	227
	350	98	399	108	467	122	542	123	583	148	581	146	609	152	723	210	564	259	926	261	895	229
Total	1413	631	1561	698	1682	749	1871	830	2099	1014	2356	1186	2545	1252	2816	1336	3105	1485	3364	1570	3516	1628

T covers all fixed capital assets.   B is the capital devoted to building and site works.

Re-evaluation of capital expenditure on school building is, however, a much more difficult operation because, in terms of school places provided, the country's post-war schools have been securing much better value for money than those built before the war.

The men and women of the Kaiser's war who became the parents of the 1920–30 school generation were promised a 'Land fit for heroes'. They received—the Geddes Axe of 1919 and the 'May report' of 1931! Those of Hitler's war having thrilled and responded to the very different promise of 'blood, toil, tears and sweat' were at least rewarded—as a result of their own exertions and a very different political climate affecting all parties—with 3,500,000 new homes and 2,600,000 new school places for their children barely fifteen years after the end of hostilities. Thus although the young parent of today is probably much more effectively vocal, and less tolerant of anything but the highest standards, than his prototype of 30 years ago, a substantial proportion at least have been able to see their children enter schools which would have appeared palatial to their own parents.

Perhaps, after all, some future historian may record that in providing and opening 3,000 new primary and over 1,600 new secondary schools within fifteen years of the end of the war despite all frustrations and handicaps, shortage of steel, shortage of traditional building materials, need to repair war damage to older buildings and shortage of building labour, the Local Education Authorities achieved a record of which the country had no need to be ashamed.

Moreover, however poorly the 'bricks-and-mortar' school of educational thought may regard our effort since 1925 it should not be forgotten that there is another side to the picture. This can best be expressed in words which Miss Horsbrugh, an unjustifiably maligned Minister, used in a speech to the Lowestoft Teachers' Association on February 5th, 1954:

> 'There are boys and girls going out from the schools today worthy of the very best this country has ever produced. There are schools that are slums and where conditions are overcrowded and appalling but where teachers are doing a real job

of work and by their skill and devotion are giving the children a really first-class education.'

Certainly, too, at no time in the educational history of this—or probably any other—country has so much first-class creative thought been devoted by architects, administrators and teachers in partnership to school design. Never before has there been such a healthy determination to ensure that every new school built shall be an emblem of fitness for purpose rather than a municipal monument, a building which shall be attractive to teachers and children alike. There have been two incidental but remarkable by-products. Firstly the pre-war ratio of teaching space to circulation space (corridors, cloakrooms, lavatories, storage, etc.) has been reversed. Before the war this was 60% circulation to 40% teaching space. It is now 60% teaching to 40% circulation. Secondly the average period of use of secondary teaching rooms has been raised from 60% to 80% of the school day. Only time can show, of course, whether, when their fabric is darkened or discoloured by age and the new spaciousness and amenities which now strike the outside observer so forcibly have become commonplace, these new schools will be regarded by our successors of the year 2000 in the same light as we regard the regrettably indestructible three deckers of the 1890's. These, too, were regarded in their day as 'handsome and worthy' structures.

It is sometimes a good corrective, too, to recall that there are still countries today—and forward-looking countries at that—where, for example, the school building regulations state almost wistfully that an effort should be made to provide every school with at least one lavatory!

Comparison of the state of public education in other countries with that in one's own is, however, a form of intellectual exercise best avoided by those who have not spent some years as teachers or administrators in close touch with the schools of the country selected. The statement that 'many of the 200 pupils hand-picked by their respective Ministries of Education to spend a year in American schools at the cost of the American Field Service had strong reservations about the academic level of the U.S.

secondary schools' is in reality meaningless. To anyone who compares the difficulties which the U.S. have had to surmount in building up their educational system with those experienced here, the point of interest is not that a handful of hand-picked pupils are critical of their standards, but that they have achieved such high standards as they have. For, starting from a population not very much larger in the 1870's than ours (U.K. 31·8 m., England and Wales 22·7 m., U.S. 38·5 m.) but spread over an area more than 50 times as great (E. & W. 58,000 sq. miles, U.S. 2,977,128 sq. miles), the U.S. have had to provide an educational system for a far-flung population which has in the interval multiplied itself by four (160 m.), while ours has barely doubled itself (E. & W. 43 m.).

They have had to weld into a sense of common nationality and way of life children representative of the most diverse racial elements, from parents speaking as their mother tongue every European and many hundreds of Asiatic, Polynesian and African languages and presenting the most diversified problems of creed, colour and physique. We by comparison have been lucky enough to have had to deal with a compact, homogeneous and sturdy child population enjoying a common history, common loyalties and traditions and basically of one creed.

Initially the problems were much the same on both sides of the Atlantic. A school place had first to be found for every child entitled to one. A respectable army of teachers had to be trained. Simultaneously a vast conscripted army of comparatively young children, few of whom knew more than a few letters of the alphabet, with ragged bodies and ragged minds, suffering from every complaint in the medical dictionary, had to have instilled into them a sense of discipline, a sense of corporate unity, ideas of hygiene and the desire to acquire the first tools of learning. Only upon the basis of these first tools—reading, writing and arithmetic—could a system of secondary and higher education be built up.

Perhaps, however, even here we were luckier than the United States in having ready for use and expansion our system of ancient secondary grammar schools and our even more ancient Universities.

A second major operation in national, regional and local planning called for by the Education Act of 1944 has been that required to train sufficient new teachers (i) to raise the school-leaving age; (ii) to replace the back-log and wastage of the war years due to retirement, deaths and the reduction of the numbers of men available for training; (iii) to eliminate unqualified teachers; and (iv) simultaneously to endeavour to reduce the size of classes in both primary and secondary schools to a point where education as distinct from the giving of formalized instruction becomes possible.

As indicated earlier in this chapter some show of defence can be offered for the country's educational building programme between the wars.

No such excuse can be put forward for our failure to train sufficient teachers during those years. In the last years before the war, the output of the grammar schools was increasing and the total number of children in the schools was in general falling. Moreover the demand for well educated young men and women from the civil and local government services, industry, the commercial world and agriculture was far less keen than it is today.

So far, however, from successive Governments making a serious attempt to eliminate unqualified teachers the national financial policy actually placed artificial restrictions on the volume of teacher training and allowed wastage to overtake replacement. A great opportunity was missed and at least half of the post-war school generation has paid the price by having to be taught in classes so large as to involve educational waste in the hands of anyone but the inevitably limited number of teachers of real genius. It is sometimes claimed by those who look at the statistics of over-large classes that a secondary class with up to 33 pupils making 90% attendance will, in fact, rarely have more than 30 children present, and that a class of 45 juniors and an average attendance of 85% becomes in effect a class of 40. Such a line of reasoning leaves out of account the essential fact that a teacher's job is concerned with the mental, moral, social and physical development of every child in her class not as a unit but as an individual.

The salient facts in the drive to raise teaching power, which has gone on in every year since the war, can be stated quite simply.

The end of the war found the country with 4,780,000 children in its schools, and 179,000 teachers. This total of children was half a million less than in 1938 but wastage during the war years had reduced the teaching force by 12,000.

In the teachers' training colleges men were being trained at little more than half the pre-war rate but the number of women entering upon courses of training was slightly higher than before the war.

Thirteen thousand entirely new teachers would be required—to raise the school-leaving age to 15—over and above what the regular training colleges could produce to replace normal wastage. Another 4,000 would be required, as a minimum, to make up for the men who would have been trained in the war years but had been in the Forces. These 17,000 and a 'windfall' of 17,000 in addition to swell the general pool were obtained by the Emergency Training Scheme. Under this scheme 34,000 men and women of excellent quality who had supplemented their education at school by the broad general education afforded by life in the Services or war work were given an intensive course of training.

If the number of children in the schools had remained stationary around the 1945 level, and had it been possible to employ in reducing the size of classes these 34,000 emergency-trained teachers together with the extra 36,000 obtained by March 1953 through the doubling of the intake to the regular training colleges, we would probably by now have been in the happy position of having no class in any school of a size much over 30.

The raising of the total teaching force by 70,000 in a matter of eight years was, of course, a remarkable feat measured by any standard and one without parallel in British educational history up to that date.

Even so late as 1948 the Ministry of Education were still optimistic enough to say in a circular (Circular 174):

'The total number of teachers is likely to match fairly closely to total requirements. There should be enough to

REPLACEMENT AND EXPANSION

enable the great majority of classes to be reduced by 1951 to a maximum of 30 for secondary schools and senior classes and 40 for primary schools and junior classes.'

Those hopes were dramatically shattered by the unprecedented number of children born in the years which followed the war.

A substantial increase in the birth-rate combined with a greatly improved survival rate may well be a cause for rejoicing from a broad national and economic standpoint. In fact, the mean birth-rates of the years 1871–75 (35·5), 1881–85 (33·3), 1886–90 (31·4), 1891–95 (30·5) and 1896–1900 (29·3) would probably have ensured a population in Great Britain sufficient to deter both the Kaiser and Hitler if they had been matched by the survival rates of today. But any such sudden increase as that which began in 1943 and has continued ever since, when combined with a reduction of the infant mortality rate in the first year of life, from 170 to 22 per 1,000, makes havoc of educational planning. Whether he is calculating his needs for additional school places or extra teachers the educational administrator feels like a man trying to race up the down staircase of an escalator!

In the years 1930–38 the number of live births had averaged 612,000. Since 1943 they have been as follows:

LIVE BIRTHS (thousands)

1943	1944	1945	1946	1947	1948	1949	1950	1951	1952	1953	1954	1955	1956	1957	1958 (provisional)
684	751	680	821	881	775	731	697	680	674	684	674	668	700	723	739

To form an estimate of the numbers from such enlarged age groups who are likely to appear on the school rolls five, ten or fifteen years later is a difficult operation. It is not merely a matter of calculating how many will survive. One must also take into account the number likely to enter direct grant and independent schools, to transfer back into the public system at some later age, and to stay on at school after fifteen.

How difficult this may become, even for the expert statisticians at the Ministry with the resources of the Government Actuary and the Registrar-General at their back, is well illustrated if one looks at the Ministry's forecasts for a few years back and compares them with the actual numbers found in the schools from year to year.

The following table shows the actual school population in maintained and assisted schools (excluding independent schools, direct grant schools, special schools and nursery schools) in various recent years; the Ministry's estimates of 1954 and revised estimates from 1959–68 published in 1958; and the teaching force available or estimated to be required in each year on the assumption that the size of classes is reduced to 30 and that the school-leaving age might be raised to 16 in 1965 as recommended by the Central Advisory Council (England) under the Chairmanship of Sir Geoffrey Crowther:

MAINTAINED AND ASSISTED PRIMARY AND SECONDARY SCHOOLS
ACTUAL AND PROJECTED NUMBER OF CHILDREN AND TEACHERS
IN THOUSANDS

Year	School Population	As projected			Total Teaching Force	If School Age raised to 16
1938	5289				191	
1945	4780				179	
1953	6056				230	
1954	6376			underestimate	232	
1955	6516	6495 ⎫		21,000 ⎫	240	
1956	6649	6608 ⎪	1954	41,000 ⎪	246	
1957	6777	6699 ⎬	projection	78,000 ⎬	253	
1958	6839	6745 ⎭		94,000 ⎭	258	
1959		6893 ⎫			263 (estimate)	
1960		6898 ⎪				
1961		6927 ⎪				
1962		6909 ⎪				
1963		6862 ⎬	1958			
1964		6861 ⎪	projection			
1965		6879 ⎪			311	332
1966		6910 ⎪			312	331
1967		6956 ⎪			314	332
1968		7016 ⎭			317	335

Columns of figures such as these tend to have the same soporific effect on any reader as Mr. McGregor's lettuces had on Peter Rabbit. Their broad implications for every one of us are, however, far too important to exclude them.

The parent concerned to discover whether teaching would be a safe (as well as a thoroughly worth-while) career for his son or daughter can see in them a guarantee that no teacher who has been accepted for training in future is likely to meet with unemployment.

The social planner must ask himself seriously whether the drain upon the very scarce and precious resources of highly qualified man and woman power in our secondary schools and Universities represented by all the teachers who will be needed can be met without taking uncomfortable and possibly drastic measures to prevent so much of it leaking away into less essential occupations through early leaving.

The proprietor of the private school can take heart from them. Provided his school can achieve recognition after inspection by the Ministry he is not likely to want for clients though he may find it increasingly difficult to obtain staff.

Even the rising business executive, who knows that 'capital' is the capacity to wait, when calculating whether he should invest his savings and bonuses or use his money in securing an education for his son at a 'Public School' (where the ratio of masters to boys will probably be twice as generous as in the local grammar schools), can feel that by so doing he may after all be helping the country in an unobtrusive way.

Although some Educational Administrators and writers in the educational press still appear to cherish a comfortable assurance that everything will come out all right after 1962 it will be noted that the 'bulge' in the birthrate between 1944 and 1949 at present appears likely to repeat itself, and that the number in the schools will reach the seven million mark for the first time in 1968. Probably, therefore, they would do well to resign themselves to the expectation that like Alice and the Red Queen they must expect to have to run as fast as they can to remain in the same place for the rest of their working lives!

No amateur student of public education should allow himself to be trapped into a discussion of the problems involved in finding the number of teachers who will be required. To contribute anything solid to such a discussion it is necessary to possess the brain of an actuary, the clairvoyance of a prophet and a profound knowledge of the precise gifts required in teaching children of widely different ages and attainments.

Wastage rates in the teaching profession are highly unpredictable. Obviously no one, even in the Ministry, can forecast a year ahead how many teachers will die, go abroad, retire early for health or other reasons or on account of marriage.

Every arbitrary assumption conceals a lurking pitfall. Suppose for example that one assumes that the profession requires twice as many women as men; that the average teaching life of a man may be put at 36–40 years and that of a woman at 18 to 20 years (allowing for those who leave on marriage); and that therefore one must train four women to every man. Every 1% by which one underestimates wastage on such an assumption can mean a 3% reduction in the surplus for which one may have been calculating. Moreover, in estimating some years ahead one has to provide for an annual increase in intake to the training colleges sufficient to repair each year's estimated wastage plus the desired surplus, plus those who may expect to fail or drop out of the training course, plus wastage on the net surplus.

Nevertheless the figures quoted above do provide a very clear indication of the magnitude of the effort which will be needed to train enough additional teachers to raise the 263,000 of 1959 to the 311,000 required to reduce the size of classes to 30 (or the 332,000 required to do this and also raise the school-leaving age) by 1965. It will be noticed that the average annual increase from 1953 to 1959 has been 5,500 a year, but that this will have to be stepped up to 8,000 a year from 1959 to 1965 to reduce the size of classes or 11,500 a year to raise the school-leaving age as well. The decision to lengthen the course of training to three years will of course mean that in 1962, the year of 'intermission', very few new teachers will be available.

Looking at the national picture as a whole it would be a mistake, too, to overlook the teachers who will be required for full-time work in the Universities and Teachers' Training Colleges; in Further Education; in Direct Grant Schools; in Special and Nursery Schools; and in Independent Schools. It will be surprising if these categories, who already numbered 68,818 in 1958, do not by 1965 swell the 335,000 required for the maintained and assisted schools to well over 400,000. On the present ratio of men to women in the teaching profession about 250,000 of the 400,000 would be women as against 150,000 men.

The normal annual wastage due to retirements, marriage and other causes in the 186,000 women teachers at work in 1958 is probably about 10,000. To raise the total to 250,000 (when wastage will become 13,000 annually) it would therefore be necessary to attract an average of 17,500 additional women into teaching each year until 1965. This would represent nearly six out of every ten of the 30,000 girls of 17, 18 and 19 at present leaving secondary schools of all types each year in England and Wales. This 30,000 includes the independent schools. By 1965 in fact of all the women employed aged between 21 and 65, no less than 1 in 24 would be a teacher.

To find the number of new men teachers required (24,000) would probably not involve so much difficulty. The annual wastage is probably not more than 3,000 in the 115,000 at present employed, but as will be seen this figure would require to be speeded up to 7,000 a year until 1965.

As has more than once been noted throughout this book, we are a very practical people capable of considerable feats of National organisation to reach any objective we desire sufficiently keenly. We organised our woman power brilliantly during Hitler's war. At one time out of 17,000,000 girls and women aged 15 to 65, no less than 9,000,000 were in full-time work for the war effort. No other combatant achieved anything at all comparable. Provided the nation has the will to do so, therefore, we could certainly implement the Crowther Report.

The omens are in fact propitious. The phenomenon of the teaching profession claiming 60% of all girls who complete a full secondary school course is not a new one, it was a common feature of the early 1950's. There are welcome signs of substantial growth in sixth-form work in the secondary schools. Recent salary improvements have combined with the arrest of inflation to make teaching a more popular option, and in fact 20,046 students have enrolled in training colleges and university training departments in 1959, as compared with 18,191 in 1958 and 15,264 in 1955. The bumper age groups of 1944, 1946, 1947 and 1948 will be reaching the age for entry to teachers' training colleges and the Universities from 1962 to 1966.

Nevertheless if we are to embark upon such a policy it would be well to recognise at the outset that unless we can find the means to keep more young women at school for a sixth-form course, we shall be ear-marking for the teaching profession such a high proportion of our precious national stock of highly trained woman power that there may be too little left for other essential professions. The nursing profession is already more than 100,000 short of what is desirable. We have only half the health visitors we need. The Younghusband Report has shown what a very large number of additional trained social workers the Welfare State is likely to require in the next few years. The professions auxiliary to the National Medical Service, such as physiotherapists, are all crying out for recruits. The civil and local government services and the banking world, which before the war were regarded as offering most desirable openings for trained women, are now glad if they can obtain a proportion of their former intake. Everyone indeed who is concerned with recruitment in such spheres as these is already encountering daily the phenomenon of too many good openings for first-class ability chasing too few candidates.

To state the problem baldly in this way is to conceal the immense difficulties its solution will present. High trainability is a delicate plant. Gaps would occur in the autumn bedding design even if every family with an intelligent child had a perfect home and the income to enjoy an appropriate standard of life. Far too many children of high intelligence still fall by the wayside through unhappy home conditions or homes actually broken by separation or divorce. The widely differing standards of access to educational opportunity—as represented by availability of good secondary schools—as between one Local Education Authority and its neighbour cry out for redress. Improved scales of maintenance allowances payable on more realistic income scales to parents prepared to keep their children at secondary schools for the vital years from 16 to 18 might stop some of the leaks. Payment of the family allowance in such cases from 16–18 might help (rather expensively) in other cases. There is, however, no sovereign remedy. Intelligent boys will continue to leave because their friends have left. Their motive may be no more than a restless itch to attain to some mental image they have formed of themselves when they come to enjoy the *status*, not always or necessarily the *wages*, of a worker. Intelligent girls will be lost to the professions because they are torn between the claims of school and the financial struggle or housekeeping fecklessness they encounter at home. Others torment themselves with a mental picture of the gulf a 'University accent' may create between themselves and their family. Others succumb to the pressure of a friend to join her in some comfortable retail distribution job because they cannot face any more the long vista of school combined with Saturday jobs and repeated spells of holiday work to help mother's struggle. The facile answer that they all get jobs anyway and can continue their education at evening classes conceals much real damage that has already been done.

Admittedly the numbers both of boys and girls remaining at school to complete a full secondary course up to 18 has in recent years been at drought level owing to the smallness of the wartime age groups and the plethora of openings. The pool will fill up again as the large age groups pass through the secondary schools. Even so it will be surprising if—with much of the machinery already to hand in the secondary schools and the Youth Employment Service—the country is not forced, within the next 15 years, to take a much firmer line to prevent early leaving except for apprenticeship in some industry which continues to give its young workers a thorough training. A policy for the annual investment of our educational capital comparable to that which, as shown earlier in this chapter, we have employed so comprehensively in investing our financial capital to increase our competitive power in the world is becoming overdue. We may, in the last resort, be forced to return to measures akin to wartime control of engagement orders and direction of labour. Any such step would certainly prove profoundly unpopular but it may be the only way to secure a continued improvement of the educational potential of the country *pari passu* with an expansion of the national productivity comparable with that of the United States, New Zealand, South Africa, Belgium and Canada.

BIBLIOGRAPHY

The following list of books and articles, while in no way comprehensive, is designed to assist the reader who may wish to follow up particular lines of inquiry suggested by the treatment of the subject adopted in this volume.

GENERAL

Education in England. W. P. Alexander. (Newnes Educational Publishing Company.)

A Hundred Years of Education. A. D. C. Peterson. (Duckworth.)

Growth in English Education. Professor H. C. Dent. (Routledge & Kegan Paul, 1954.)

Looking Forward in Education. A symposium edited by Professor A. V. Judges. (Faber & Faber, 1955.)

Education and the Democratic Ideal. Dr. A. G. Hughes. (Longman's Green, 1951.)

The Silent Social Revolution. An account of the expansion of Public Education in England and Wales, 1895–1935. G. A. N. Lowndes. (Oxford University Press, 1937.)

Ten Years of Change. Report of the West Riding Education Committee.

To Whom Do the Schools Belong? W. O. Lester Smith, 1945. (Blackwell.)

Broadsheets. No. 358, Schools under Pressure. The Shortage of Teachers.

No. 359, Building and Costs. (P.E.P., 16 Queen Anne's Gate, S.W.1.)

The Cost of Education. Do We Get Value for Money? Three Articles in *Education.* W. P. Alexander. June 12th, 19th and 25th, 1953.

The Costs of Education. John Vaizey. (Allen & Unwin, 1958.)

PRIMARY EDUCATION

(i) Official publications

Primary Education. Suggestions for Teachers. (H.M.S.O., 1959.)

Seven to Eleven. Educational Pamphlet, No. 15. (H.M.S.O.)

The Story of a School. Educational Pamphlet, No. 14. (H.M.S.O.)

Moving and Growing. Physical Education in the Primary School. (H.M.S.O.)

The Primary School Report of the Consultative Committee of the Board of Education, 1931. (H.M.S.O.)

Primary Education. Report of the Advisory Council on Education in Scotland, 1947.

(ii) Individual works

Testing Results in the Infant School. D. E. M. Gardner. (Methuen.)

Long-Term Results of Infant School Methods, 1950. D. E. M. Gardner. (Methuen.)

Activity in the Primary School. M. V. Daniell, 1947. (Blackwell.)

Purpose in the Junior School. W. K. Richmond, 1949. (Redman.)

Junior School Community. M. Atkinson, 1949. (Longmans.)

Nursery—Infant Education. National Union of Teachers, 1949. (Evans Bros.)

Trends in Primary Education. London County Council, 1950.

SECONDARY EDUCATION

(i) Official publications

1947, *The New Secondary Education.* Educational Pamphlet, No. 9. (H.M.S.O.)

1947, *Report of the Advisory Council* on Education in Scotland on Secondary Education.

1947, *School and Life.* Report of the Central Advisory Council for Education.

1959, *15 to 18.* Report of the Central Advisory Council for Education in England. (The Crowther Report, H.M.S.O.)

(ii) Individual works

Education and Social Change. F. Clark, 1940. (Sheldon Press.)
Secondary Education for All. H. C. Dent, 1949. (Routledge and Kegan Paul Ltd.)
The Future in Education. Sir R. Livingstone, 1941. (Cambridge University Press.)
The Education of Girls. J. Newsom, 1948. (Faber.)
The Nation's Secondary Schools, Assistant Masters' Association, 1946. (I.A.A.M., 29 Gordon Square, W.C.1.)
The Organization of Comprehensive Schools. London County Council, County Hall. (Staples Press.)
Inside the Comprehensive Schools. A symposium by Heads. (Schoolmaster Publishing Co., 1958.)
Comprehensive Schools Today. Interim survey with critical Essays. Dr. Robin Pedley. (Councils and Education Press.)
Comprehensive Education. A new approach. Dr. Robin Pedley. (Gollancz, 1956.)
The Leicestershire Experiment. Stewart C. Mason. (Councils and Education Press, 1957.)
Secondary Modern Schools. Professor H. C. Dent. (Routledge, 1958.)
Your Secondary Modern Schools. J. Vincent Chapman. (College of Preceptors, 1959.)
The Choice Before Us. Alternatives to 11-plus. *Times Educational Supplement.* Feb. 6, 1959. Articles by Dr. Robin Pedley.

TECHNOLOGICAL AND FURTHER EDUCATION

Recent advance has been so rapid that I know of no volume which conveys an up-to-date and comprehensive picture. *The Times* supplement *Technology* is invaluable and always stimulating.

Recent works which the student will wish to study are:

Technical Education and Social Changes. Stephen Cotgrove. (Allen & Unwin.)
On Being a Technologist. Professor D. G. Christopherson. (S.C.M. Press, 1959.)

Recruitment to Skilled Trades. Lady G. Williams. (Routledge & Kegan Paul, 1957.)

Scientific and Engineering Manpower in Great Britain 1959. Cmd. 902, H.M.S.O.)
An American study of the British educational system and social and economic factors affecting the manpower situation is in preparation. It will be *Britain's Scientific and Technological Manpower* by G. L. Payne. (Stanford University Press.)

The report on Universities and Industry published by the Anglo-American Council of Productivity is purchasable at 21 Tothill Street, S.W.1.

THE WELFARE SERVICES OF EDUCATION

(i) Official Publications

A comprehensive picture can be obtained only by a study of the Annual Reports of the Chief Medical Officer of the Ministry of Education on 'The Health of the School Child', published by H.M.S.O., and the Annual Reports of County and County Borough School Medical Officers.

Report on the Training of Health Visitors. (H.M.S.O., 1956.)
The Training of Social Workers. (The Younghusband Report, H.M.S.O., 1959.)

(ii) Individual Works

The School Health Service by S. Leff, M.D., D.P.H., and Vera Leff. (H. K. Lewis & Co., 1959.)

INDEX

Adult Education, 74, 102, 103
Age of entry to school, 139
Agriculture, 100, 160
Analysis of children's mental content, 19, 75
Ancient Grammar Schools, 105, 166
Animals, as teaching material, 19

Bevin, Mr. Ernest, 77, 78
Birth rate, 158, 169
'Black List' of school buildings, 154
Blind children, 120, 121
Boots and clothing, 104, 144
Bryce, Lord, 34
Building labour, 155–8
Burnham, salary scales, 82, 172

Capital investment (national), 159–64
Central Scientific and Technical Register (Ministry of Labour), 99
Child growth and behaviour, 16–23
Guidance Clinics, 15, 104, 130–3
Churchill, Sir Winston, 35, 81
City and Guilds of London, examinations, 75, 94
Classes, reductions in size of, 149, 157, 172
Cleary, Sir William, 160, 162
Clothing of schoolchildren, 104, 148
Co-education, 32
Colleges of Advanced Technology, 88, 90
Comprehensive schools, 53–7
Continental journeys, 55, 145
Crowther Report, 170–4

Daytime release of young employees, 77–9
Deafness in children, 122, 123

Design of schools, 165
Diabetes in children, 125, 126
Dinners, school, 104, 116
Diphtheria, 108
Diploma in Technology, 90, 91
Diseases of childhood, deaths from, 107, 109
Dramatic sense in young children, 22
Dutch East Indies, 141

Education Act, 1902, 143
1944, 31, 35, 51, 149
for leisure, 99
Educational press, 26
Educationally sub-normal children, 127–9
Eighteen-plus problems, 60
Eleven, the break at, 30, 51–3
Emergency Teachers' Training Scheme, 168
Epileptic children, 126
Equipment in schools, 149
Exchequer share of cost of public education, 152
Experiment in teaching methods, 25

Family allowances, 174
Federation of secondary modern schools, 48
Freedom and activity, 25–7
enjoyed by head teachers, 26

General Certificate of Education, 41
German Continuation Schools, 77
Government Evacuation Scheme, 107, 130, 154

'Hadow' Report on the Education of the Adolescent, 1926, 31
Handicapped children, 118–33

Health Visitors, 114
'High School' solution, the, 57–9
History, introduction to, 20
Horsbrugh, Miss Florence, 164
Housing, 110, 154, 164
Humphry Ward, Mrs., 107

INDUSTRIAL Revolution, the second, 36, 82, 85
Inspectorate of Schools, Her Majesty's, 25, 27

JOHNSON, Doctor, 140

LEAVING age, minimum, 31
    in the U.S.A., 77
Leicestershire experiment, 57–9
London 'Care Committee Organization', 115

McMILLAN, Miss Margaret, 26, 29
Maintenance allowances, 174
Maladjustment in children, 130–3
Malnutrition, 107, 108
Maternity and Child Welfare, 108
Mathematics, introduction to, 13, 17
Milk in schools, 104, 124
Minor Ailments Clinics, 111
Montessori, Madame, 26
Museum cupboards, 18, 145

NATIONAL Apprenticeship Council, 78
    Certificate Courses, 80
    Colleges of Technology, 73
    Health Service, 111–13
Newman, Cardinal, 70
    Sir George, 107, 133
Nuffield Provincial Hospitals' Trust, 114
Nursery schools, 27, 61

OWEN, Robert, 106

PARENTAL influences, 51
Partially-sighted children, 121
    deaf children, 123

Part-time release classes, 78
Penny dinners, 106
'Percy' Committees, 84
Phenylketonuria, 129
Photographs of children at different epochs, 147
Physical education, 21, 145
Physically handicapped children, 123–5
Pictures in schools, 146
Poliomyelitis, 109, 118
Primary School: today's objective, 16; yesterday's objective, 24
Private schools, 139, 140, 171
Psychology and the Child, 14
Public Schools, the, 138, 171

RAISING school-leaving age to 16, 172
Rate-borne cost of public education, 152
Reading ability, 46
Re-capitulation of racial memories, theory of, 23
Recruitment to the professions, 174
Refresher courses for teachers, 26
Remodelling of old school buildings, 155
Replacement of old schools, 155
Research into children's educational needs at various ages, 15
    movement and growth, 21
Resources of highly trainable man- and woman-power, 174
Rickets, disappearance of, 118

SADLER, Sir Michael, 34
'Sandwich' courses, 91
School:
    Camps, 145
    Dental Service, 113
    Meals, 116
    Medical Officers, 111
    Medical Service, 110
Secondary Education, function of, 32
    objectives, of, 33
    grammar schools, 39–42
    modern schools, 45–51
    technical schools, 35, 42–5

Single sex education, 31
Social influence of public education, 148
Spastics, 124
Special schools, 118–33
Stammering in children, 133
State scholarships, 63, 68, 92
Sunshine Homes for Blind Babies, 120

TAWNEY, Professor R. H., 35
Teachers' training colleges, 28, 29
Teaching profession:
    increase in numbers, 172
    progressive improvement of standards, 148
    training problems, 171
Technologists, output of, 86
    Russian, 85
Tests of academic aptitude, 127, 141
Transference, theory of, 22

UNESCO, 46

United States of America:
    'Comprehensive' schools in, 54
    Educational achievement of, 166
    University education in, 77, 85
Universities:
    expansion of, 60–2
    numbers in attendance at, 61
    proportion of each age group attaining, 66
    sources of income, 64
    trends in development, 62

VOLUNTARY effort by pioneers, 106
    workers in London, 115

WAR damage to housing, 157
    to schools, 157
Webb, Mr. Sidney, 34
Welfare, foods, 110
Women and girls, proportion in employment, 77, 173

YOUTH Employment Service, 119, 175